LISTENING POWER 1

Language Focus • Comprehension Focus • Listening for Pleasure

Bruce Rogers

Dorothy Zemach

PEARSON
Longman

Listening Power 1

Pearson Education, 10 Bank Street, White Plains, NY 10606

Staff credits: The people who made up the *Listening Power* team, representing editorial, production, design, manufacturing, and marketing are John Brezinsky, Dave Dickey, Nancy Flaggman, Ann France, Amy McCormick, Liza Pleva, Jaimie Scanlon, Loretta Steeves, and Paula Van Ells.

Test composition: TSI Graphics
Text font: 12.5/14 Adobe Caslon
Illustrations: TSI Graphics
Credits: See page 119.

Library of Congress Cataloging-in-Publication Data
Rogers, Bruce
  Listening power. 1: language focus: comprehension focus: listening for pleasure/Bruce Rogers, Dorothy Zemach.
    p. cm.
  ISBN 0-13-611421-0—ISBN 0-13-611425-3—ISBN 0-13-611428-8
  1. English language—Textbooks for foreign speakers. 2. Listening. 3. Reading comprehension.
I. Zemach, Dorothy II. Title.
  PE1128.R63446 2011
  428.3 4–dc22
                                                                    2010043222

ISBN-10: 0-13-611421-0
ISBN-13: 978-0-13-611421-5

Printed in the United States of America
2 3 4 5 6 7 8 9 10—V042—15 14 13 12 11

Contents

Acknowledgments

The authors of *Listening Power 1* would like to thank Amy McCormick for her guiding vision for the book and the series; Jaimie Scanlon for her skillful and thorough editing of the manuscript; Loretta Steeves for her work in shaping the project and bringing it to completion; our fellow *Listening Power* authors David Bohlke and Tammy LeRoi Gilbert for their feedback, suggestions, and encouragement. We'd also like to thank the entire staff at Pearson Longman for a job well done.

The authors and publisher would also like to extend special thanks to the following teachers around the world who reviewed the *Listening Power* series and provided indispensable feedback.

Abigail Brown, Assistant Professor, TransPacific Hawaii College; Alison Evans, Senior Instructor, University of Oregon; Amy Christensen, Instructor, Central New Mexico Community College; Matthew Fryslie, Instructor, Kainan University; Ian K. Leighton, Instructor, SungKyun Language Institute; Rosa Vasquez, Instructor, John F. Kennedy Institute of Languages.

Bruce Rogers   Boulder, Colorado
Dorothy Zemach   Eugene, Oregon

About the Authors

Bruce Rogers has taught language and test preparation courses to English language learners since 1979. He taught at the Economics Institute, University of Colorado, Boulder for twenty-one years. He has also taught in Indonesia, Vietnam, Korea, and the Czech Republic. He is the author of six other textbooks for English language learners and is the past president of Colorado TESOL. He lives and works in Boulder, Colorado, USA.

Dorothy Zemach is a materials writer, editor, and teacher trainer specializing in English language learning and teaching. She lives in Eugene, Oregon, and has taught for over twenty years in language schools and universities in the US, Asia, and the Middle East. Dorothy is a frequent presenter at international conferences. She is the author or co-author of over fifteen textbooks for English language learners.

Introduction to *Listening Power 1*

To the Teacher

Helping students develop strong listening skills is an important part of any language program. Good listening skills are a necessity in the classroom and the workplace, as well as in social interactions. In addition, standard English-language tests, such as TOEFL©, TOEIC©, and IELTS©, also require solid skills in listening. Listening was once considered a passive skill, but research has shown that successful listening requires the listener's active engagement. Listening is also considered by many learners to be the most challenging language skill.

The *Listening Power* series is designed to help learners meet the challenges of listening in English and provide students with the effective listening strategies that they need. It also provides a wealth of practice materials designed to facilitate listening fluency.

Listening Power 1 has three separate parts, each related to one of three important elements of effective listening. Unlike other listening skills programs, *Listening Power* does not require classes to begin with the first unit and work their way page by page to the end. Teachers and students are encouraged to skip from part to part and unit to unit.

Part 1: Language Focus—The units in this section target specific language skill areas that are often challenging for learners when they listen. These include understanding various types of questions, understanding numbers and time expressions, and understanding contractions. After each **Skill Presentation**, there is a set of practice activities, followed by the **Put It Together** section, which provides consolidated practice with longer, more challenging listenings centered on an interesting topic or theme. Teachers may choose to have students complete Put It Together exercises immediately after completing the skill sections or use them for later review.

Part 2: Comprehension Focus—This part of the text includes two sub-sections. The units in the **Building Skills** section present skills required to comprehend longer conversations and lectures, such as understanding main ideas, supporting ideas, and details; making inferences; and separating opinions from facts. Each Building Skills unit includes integrated practice activities. The **Applying Skills** units offer high-interest, theme-based listening texts and additional practice activities designed to help students put their new skills to practical use.

Part 3: Listening For Pleasure—This part of the book is just for fun! Lessons are designed to build students' confidence in listening by presenting enjoyable, motivating topics and contexts, such as TV shows and stories. These lessons can be used at any time during the course to provide a change of pace and to show students that listening can be interesting and pleasurable.

Although the unit structure varies somewhat from part to part, most of the longer listenings follow this pattern:

Unit Warm Up: These activities activate students' prior knowledge of the topic.

Before You Listen: This section includes a **Vocabulary Preview** which targets high-frequency, useful words from the listening text. In addition, students have an opportunity to predict the listening content.

While You Listen: Students listen and complete one or more tasks which practice what they learned in the Skill Presentation.

After You Listen: These activities integrate speaking to reinforce the target listening skills. Tasks are designed to stimulate discussion and critical thinking about issues raised in the listening.

A wide variety of topics are discussed in *Listening Power*. All were chosen to be engaging and of high interest to as many learners as possible.

The authors of the *Listening Power* series hope that both you and your students find this series useful and enjoyable.

To the Student

Welcome to Listening Power!

Listening is a very important language skill. Most people spend more time listening than they do speaking, reading or writing. Listening is important in the classroom, at work, and in social situations. However, learning to listen in another language can be difficult. When you listen to a TV show, movie, lecture, or conversation in English, you may feel overwhelmed and "tune out" (stop listening).

Listening Power will help you improve your listening skills. You'll practice listening to sentences, short conversations, longer dialogs, mini-lectures, and parts of radio and TV shows. As you listen, you'll complete different types of activities to help you build useful vocabulary and understand and respond to what you hear in English.

In class, you will work on your own, in pairs or groups, and as a whole class. To get the most out of this course, you need to relax and focus on just listening. Don't worry if you don't understand everything that you hear or if you cannot complete an activity. If you have problems, ask your teacher to repeat a listening or help you with the activity.

Listening Power 1 has three parts, so it is like three books in one. However, you do not have to complete the parts in order. You and your teacher are encouraged to work on more than one listening skill at one time, and to practice the skills that you and your classmates need most.

Part 1: Language Focus—The units in this part of the book focus on challenging language skill areas. For example, you'll listen to different types of questions, statements involving numbers and letters, and time expressions.

Part 2: Comprehension Focus—In this part, you will listen to longer conversations and mini-lectures, and practice important listening skills, such as understanding main ideas and details and making inferences. The **Applying Skills** units at the end of Part 2 offer interesting listening texts and additional practice activities to help you use your new listening skills.

Part 3: Listening For Pleasure—These lessons will allow you to enjoy listening to folk stories and parts of TV shows in English as you build your listening skills.

To really improve your listening skills, the authors recommend that you try to listen to English as much as possible and use your English whenever you can. Listen to the radio, and watch television shows and movies in English. Take part in conversations in English, and visit Internet sites that provide practice listening to English.

We hope that you find this series useful and enjoyable.

Bruce Rogers
Dorothy Zemach

PART 1

Language Focus

Understanding *Wh-Questions*

Unit Warm Up

Work with a partner. Look at the picture. What are the people doing? What questions do you think they are asking? Use the words below to help you.

Who...? What...? Where...? When...? Why...? How...? Which...?

SKILL PRESENTATION

Wh- Questions

Many questions in English begin with question words that start with *Wh-*: *Who, What, Where, When, Why* and *Which*. Sometimes these are called "information questions," because the *Wh-* words ask for different kinds of information. We can also include the question word *How* with the other *Wh-* question words.

When you understand what kind of information the speaker is looking for, it's easier to understand how to answer.

A. 🎧 *Listen to the questions and responses.*

Questions	Responses
1. Who are you calling?	Steve. It's his birthday today.
2. What do you call this in English?	A stapler.
3. What time does the movie start?	The late show starts at 9:30.
4. Where does the #18 bus go?	I think it goes to the mall.
5. When is your birthday?	It's October 27th.
6. Why are you late?	Because I missed the train.
7. Which Chinese restaurant do you like best?	Jade Palace. It's great.
8. How do you turn on the printer?	Press this button here.
9. How often do you go to the gym?	Three times a week.
10. How much does that phone cost?	It's about $100.
11. How about ordering a pizza?	That sounds great.

B. 🎧 *Listen and repeat the questions.*

A. Match the question words or phrases to the type of information they ask about.

_____ 1. Who

_____ 2. What

_____ 3. Where

_____ 4. When

_____ 5. Why

_____ 6. Which

_____ 7. How

_____ 8. How often

_____ 9. How much/many

a. a reason

b. a time or date

c. a fact; the name of something

d. a person

e. the way something happens

f. a place

g. one thing/choice from a group of more than one

h. an amount or a number

i. the number of times something happens

B. Complete the questions. Then ask and answer them with a partner. More than one answer may be possible for some items.

1. _____ do you live?

2. _____ is your last name?

3. _____ brothers and sisters do you have?

4. _____ does this class finish?

5. _____ is your favorite sport to play?

6. _____ is your favorite actor?

7. _____ do you eat in restaurants?

8. _____ is the nearest bus stop?

9. _____ is your English teacher?

10. _____ are you studying English?

Wh- Questions and Intonation

In English, both statements and *Wh-* questions end with falling intonation. With *Wh-* questions, the speaker's voice typically rises and then falls at the very end of the sentence. You need to listen carefully. The *Wh-* word at the beginning tells you the speaker has asked a question.

A. 🎧 *Listen to the questions and responses.*

Questions	Responses
1. When is your birthday?	It's October 27th.
2. Where does the number 18 bus go?	I think it goes to the mall.
3. Who are you calling?	Steve. It's his birthday today.
4. What time does the movie start?	The late show starts at 9:30.

B. 🎧 *Listen and repeat the questions.*

☑ Check Yourself

A. 🎧 *Listen. Do you hear a* **Wh-** *question or a statement? Check (✓) your answers in the boxes at the left.*

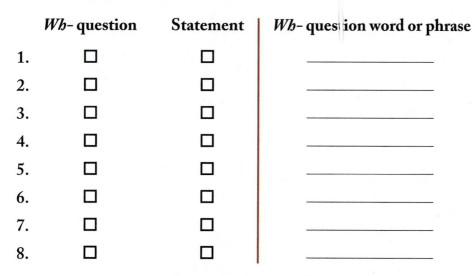

	Wh- question	Statement	*Wh-* question word or phrase
1.	☐	☐	_____
2.	☐	☐	_____
3.	☐	☐	_____
4.	☐	☐	_____
5.	☐	☐	_____
6.	☐	☐	_____
7.	☐	☐	_____
8.	☐	☐	_____

B. 🎧 *Listen again. For each* **Wh-** *question in Exercise A, write the* **Wh-** *question word or phrase that you hear.*

When You Don't Understand

In conversation, when you hear a *Wh-* question word and the falling intonation at the end of the sentence, you know that the speaker asked you a question, and you need to give an answer.

With *Wh-* questions, you can't answer by saying just "Yes" or "No." It's important to understand the question, so you can answer with the correct information.

Here are some ways you can ask for help when you don't understand the question.

> **Note**
> It's polite to begin with *I'm sorry* when you ask the speaker to repeat information.

A. 🎧 *Listen to the questions and responses.*

Questions	Responses
	I'm sorry, ...
1. Who's your favorite actor?	Could you say that again?
2. How often do you eat out?	I don't understand the question.
3. What time is your appointment?	Could you say that another way?
4. Excuse me. Where's the library?	Where is the...?
5. Why didn't you call me?	Why didn't I...?

B. 🎧 *Listen and repeat the responses.*

☑ **Check Yourself**

🎧 *Listen. Circle the response that you hear.*

1. (a.) What did you ask?　　　b. What time is the...?

2. a. I don't understand.　　　b. Could you say that again?

3. a. Who is the...?　　　b. How is the...?

4. a. I don't know the answer.　　　b. I don't understand the question.

5. a. Could you say that again?　　　b. Could you say that another way?

6. a. Who is the...?　　　b. What's the...?

PRACTICE

■ EXERCISE 1

A. Read the conversations. Use Wh- words to complete the questions.

1.

A: Hi, Jenny. _____ were you yesterday?

B: Oh, I was sick. _____ did I miss?

A: We corrected the homework, and then reviewed for the chapter test.

B: A test? Oh, no, _____ is it?

A: It's today.

2.

A: Excuse me. How much does this dress cost?

B: Let's see… that's $179.

A: Wow! _____ is it so expensive?

B: Because it's one of our new spring styles.

A: I see. _____ about the blue one?

B: That's on sale, for $59. We only have a few sizes left. _____ size are you?

A: I'm a medium. _____ can I try this on?

B: The dressing rooms are over there.

B. 🎧 **Listen to the conversations from Exercise A. Pay attention to the intonation. Then practice the conversations with a partner.**

■ EXERCISE 2

A. 🎧 **Close your eyes. Listen to the questions. Think about what kind of information the speaker is asking for.**

B. 🎧 **Listen again. Check (✓) the best answers.**

1. ☐ Every day.   ☐ At 3:40.
2. ☐ With a friend.   ☐ A dance class.
3. ☐ It's me - Jennifer.   ☐ 555-8120.
4. ☐ Three or four times a week. ☐ At the university.
5. ☐ $49.95.   ☐ It's dark blue.

(continued)

6. ☐ My brother.   ☐ Yesterday, I think.

7. ☐ About $17 for a large pizza.   ☐ Papa's Pizza Parlor.

8. ☐ This black one.   ☐ It can play movies too.

C. 🎧 *Listen to the full conversations and check your answers.*

■ EXERCISE 3

🎧 *Listen to the conversation. Circle the best response to the question.*

1. a. My name is Ben.
   b. I'm fine, thank you.
   c. It's nice to meet you too.

2. a. Just around the corner.
   b. I don't like coffee.
   c. It's about $3.00.

3. a. The Coffee Break.
   b. At about 1:00.
   c. I'm sorry. Why is it...?

4. a. Once or twice a week.
   b. Because I'm late.
   c. They have really good food.

5. a. He's a waiter.
   b. I go there for lunch.
   c. Sandwiches and salads.

6. a. The burgers are great.
   b. Three or four dollars.
   c. They're very kind.

■ EXERCISE 4

A. 🎧 *Listen to the conversations. Check the questions you hear.*

1. ☐ What's your name?
   ☐ How are you?
   ☐ Where are you from?
   ☐ What's your major?

2. ☐ What movie is playing?
   ☐ Where is Lisa?
   ☐ What time does the movie start?
   ☐ Why is she always late?

3. ☐ Where should we eat?
   ☐ What are you going to have?
   ☐ What am I going to...?
   ☐ Who's coming to lunch?

4. ☐ How do you spell that?

    ☐ What's your occupation, Ms. Kang?

    ☐ Where do you live?

    ☐ What do you do?

B. 🎧 *Listen to each conversation again. Circle the correct word to complete the sentence.*

1. Maria is taking *(English / Business / Spanish)* classes now.

2. Their friend Lisa is *(at home / late / on the bus)*.

3. The woman is going to drink *(coffee / lemonade / tea)*.

4. Ms. Kang works *(at a bank / at a school / at a doctor's office)*.

■ EXERCISE 5

A. 🎧 *Listen. Write the* Wh- *question word or phrase that you hear.*

1. _____

2. _____

3. _____

4. _____

5. _____

6. _____

7. _____

8. _____

B. 🎧 *Listen again. Write your answers to the questions.*

1. _____

2. _____

3. _____

4. _____

5. _____

6. _____

7. _____

8. _____

PUT IT TOGETHER

Polite Questions

Different cultures have different ideas about questions. For example, in some cultures, asking "How old are you?" can seem like a very personal question. But, in other cultures, it's perfectly OK to ask a person's age.

Even in the same country, different groups of people ask different questions. For example, you can ask your friends more personal questions than you can ask your boss, your teacher, or someone you just met.

Remember that you don't have to answer a question just because someone asks it. You can say, politely, "Sorry, I'd rather not say," or you can just smile and say, "That's a personal question."

■ EXERCISE 1

A. Vocabulary Preview *Check these words in a dictionary. Write **P** if they have a positive (good) meaning, and **N** if they have a negative (bad) meaning. Then discuss your answers with a partner.*

_____ appropriate   _____ nosy

_____ curious   _____ polite

_____ inappropriate   _____ rude

B. 🎧 *Listen to each conversation. Circle the question the people are talking about.*

1. a. How old are you?

   b. How many children do you have?

2. a. Why did you leave your last job?

   b. Why don't you have a job?

3. a. What's your last name?

   b. What's your salary?

4. a. How many children do you want to have?

   b. How many children do you have?

5. a. What's your address?

   b. What's your email address?

C. 🎧 *Listen again. What do the people think about the questions? Circle ok or not ok for each person.*

	Man		Woman	
1.	ok	not ok	ok	not ok
2.	ok	not ok	ok	not ok
3.	ok	not ok	ok	not ok
4.	ok	not ok	ok	not ok
5.	ok	not ok	ok	not ok

■ EXERCISE 2

🎧 *Listen. Does the person feel the question was ok or not ok? Did the person answer or not answer? Check (✓) the columns.*

	OK	Not OK	Answered	Didn't Answer
1.				
2.				
3.				
4.				
5.				

■ EXERCISE 3

A. *Are these questions OK to ask a stranger? Are they OK to ask a friend? Check (✓) the appropriate column.*

		Stranger	Friend
1.	How old are you?	☐	☐
2.	How many children do you want?	☐	☐
3.	Where does your family live?	☐	☐
4.	What's your email address?	☐	☐
5.	What grade did you get on the English test?	☐	☐
6.	Why are you late?	☐	☐
7.	What's your favorite restaurant?	☐	☐
8.	Who is your hero?	☐	☐

B. Share your answers to Exercise A with a partner. Explain your choices.

Examples

> *I think it's OK to ask, "How old are you?" to a friend but not a stranger. A stranger might not want to tell their age.*
>
> *It's rude to ask, "What grade did you get?" to a stranger because...*

C. Work with a group. Discuss the questions.

1. What are some questions you ask people when you first meet them? What are some questions you hope people will ask you?

2. What are some questions that are OK to ask...
   - a child, but not an adult?
   - an adult, but not a child?
   - a family member, but not a friend?
   - a co-worker, but not your boss?
   - a classmate, but not your teacher?

3. What do you do or say when someone asks you a question you don't want to answer?

D. Work with a partner. Write some questions that are OK to ask classmates. Then join another pair. Ask and answer each other's questions.

Understanding Yes/No and Alternative Questions

Unit Warm Up

A. Work with a partner. Look at the pictures. What questions do you think the people are asking? Use the phrases below to help you.

Can I... ?   Is this...?   Are you...?   Do you...?   Did you...?   Is there...?

B. Join another pair and share your questions.

SKILL PRESENTATION

Yes/No Questions

Yes/No questions ask for an answer of *yes* or *no*. These questions begin with auxiliary verbs such as *do/does/did*, *will*, or *can*. A yes/no question can also begin with a form of the main verb *be*.

One way to answer yes/no questions is with short answers, either affirmative (*yes*) or negative (*no*).

Read the examples in the chart. Notice how yes/no questions are formed from statements and how to answer in the affirmative and negative.

What do you notice about the order of the subjects and verbs in the question forms?

Look at the last two questions. What auxiliary verb do we use to form yes/no questions?

Statements	Yes/No Questions	Short Answers
Rose is a doctor.	Is Rose a doctor?	Yes, she is. / No, she isn't.
Michael can understand German.	Can Michael understand German?	Yes, he can. / No, he can't.
There was a fire at the school.	Was there a fire at the school?	Yes, there was. / No, there wasn't.
It is raining.	Is it raining?	Yes, it is. / No, it isn't.
You like action movies.	Do you like action movies?	Yes, I do. / No, I don't.
Professor Mondello went to the meeting.	Did Professor Mondello go to the meeting?	Yes, he did. / No, he didn't.

A. 🎧 *Listen to the questions and responses.*

Questions	Responses
1. Do you like this weather?	**Yes, I do.** It's beautiful.
2. Can you swim?	**Yes, I can.** I love swimming.
3. Are these your notes?	**No, they aren't.** I think they're Karen's.
4. Is her name Daniela?	**Yes, it is.** Daniela Smith.
5. Are there any new students in the class?	**No, there aren't.** They're the same students that were in class last term.

B. 🎧 *Listen and repeat the questions.*

A. *Work with a partner. Change these statements into yes/no questions. Then write the affirmative and negative short answers.*

1. You enjoy this class.	<u> *Do you enjoy this class?* </u> <u> *Yes, I Do.* </u> / <u> *No, I don't.* </u>
2. You are from the U.S.	_____ _____ / _____
3. It rained yesterday.	_____ ? _____ / _____
4. Your cell phone is new.	_____ ? _____ / _____
5. Your family lives nearby.	_____ ? _____ / _____
6. You drive to school every day.	_____ ? _____ / _____
7. You can speak Spanish.	_____ ? _____ / _____
8. There is an English test tomorrow.	_____ ? _____ / _____

B. *Take turns asking the questions from Exercise A. Give your own short answers.*

Yes/No Questions and Intonation

The intonation of yes/no questions is different from *Wh-* questions (See Part 1, Unit 1, page 5). *Wh-* questions have falling intonation (the voice goes down at the end). In yes/no questions, the voice rises (goes up) at the end.

🎧 *Listen and repeat the questions.*

1. Do you like chocolate?

2. Is there a problem?

3. Can you fix my computer?

4. Did Robert move to an apartment?

5. Were they at the library?

🎧 *Listen to the conversations. Do you hear a statement, a yes/no question, or a Wh- question? Check (✓) your answers.*

	Statement	Yes/No Question	*Wh-* Question
1.	☐	☐	☐
2.	☐	☐	☐
3.	☐	☐	☐
4.	☐	☐	☐
5.	☐	☐	☐
6.	☐	☐	☐

Other Ways to Answer Yes/No Questions

Besides short answers, you may hear speakers answer yes/no questions in other ways. There are many ways to say *yes* or *no*, and sometimes answers are not affirmative or negative. For example, a person can say, "Maybe" or "I don't know." It's useful to understand these other types of responses to yes/no questions.

Question: *Do you want to go to Martin's party?*

Affirmative Responses	Negative Responses	Other Responses
I think so.	I don't think so.	Maybe.
Of course.	I'm afraid not.	I don't know.
Definitely.	Probably not.	I'm not sure.

A. 🎧 *Listen to the questions and responses.*

Questions	Responses
1. Do you enjoy this music?	I'm afraid not.
2. Did Matthew tell you the news?	Of course.
3. Do they know how to cook?	I'm not sure.
4. Is he ready to go now?	I don't think so.
5. Will the concert start on time?	Probably not.
6. Will the bus come soon?	Maybe.

B. 🎧 *Listen and repeat the responses.*

☑ Check Yourself

🎧 *Listen and check (✓) the type of response that you hear.*

	Affirmative	Negative	Other
1.	☐	☐	☐
2.	☐	☐	☐
3.	☐	☐	☐
4.	☐	☐	☐
5.	☐	☐	☐
6.	☐	☐	☐

Alternative Questions

Alternative questions ask about two choices or possibilities. These questions always have the word *or*.

> Do you want coffee *or* tea?

> Will you take the 1:00 train *or* the 3:00 train?

> Was the English test easy *or* difficult?

Note

• To answer an alternative question, you need to name one of the choices. It is NOT correct to answer an alternative question *yes* or *no*.

> Do you want coffee or tea?
>> ✓ *Tea, please.* (CORRECT)
>> ✗ *Yes, I do.* (INCORRECT)

• The intonation of an alternative question usually rises for the first choice and then falls for the second choice:

> Do you want coffee or tea?

A. 🎧 *Listen to the questions and responses.*

Questions	Responses
1. Do you prefer to watch basketball or baseball?	I prefer baseball.
2. Does Mr. Kim live alone or with a roommate?	He lives alone.
3. Is your English class in the morning or in the afternoon?	In the morning.
4. Are you studying Spanish or French?	I'm studying French.
5. Did they eat at home or go to a restaurant last night?	They went out.

B. 🎧 *Listen and repeat the questions.*

☑ **Check Yourself**

🎧 *Listen. Do you hear a yes/no question or an alternative question?*
Check (✓) your answers.

	Yes/No	Alternative
1.	☐	☐
2.	☐	☐
3.	☐	☐
4.	☐	☐
5.	☐	☐
6.	☐	☐

PRACTICE

■ **EXERCISE 1**

🎧 *Listen. Write the number of each question next to the correct short answer.*

____ **a.** Yes, I do.

____ **b.** Yes, they were.

____ **c.** No, I didn't.

____ **d.** No, you can't.

____ **e.** Yes, I am.

____ **f.** No, she isn't.

____ **g.** Yes, it did.

____ **h.** No, there aren't.

🎧 *Listen and write answers to the questions. Don't use the words* yes *or* no *in your answers.*

1. _____
2. _____
3. _____
4. _____
5. _____
6. _____
7. _____

EXERCISE 3

Match the two halves of each question. Then ask and answer the questions with a partner.

_____ 1. Are you from a big city   a. or a shower?

_____ 2. Is your family large   b. or pop music?

_____ 3. Do you prefer rock   c. or an apartment?

_____ 4. Do you live in a house   d. or a small town?

_____ 5. Do you usually take a bath   e. or small?

_____ 6. In your country, is it warm   f. or cold at this time of year?

EXERCISE 4

🎧 *Listen. Circle the best response to complete each conversation.*

1. a. I'll have the pasta.
   b. Yes, please.
   c. Soup, please.

2. a. I don't know.
   b. No, thank you.
   c. Cats and dogs.

3. a. No. Just really tired.
   b. At the library.
   c. With my friends.

4. a. Fruit sounds good.
   b. Yes, I do.
   c. In about an hour.

5. a. They bought it last week.
   b. No, it wasn't.
   c. It's used.

6. a. On the radio.
   b. No, I read it on the Internet.
   c. No, it's going to rain.

(continued)

Understanding Yes/No and Alternative Questions   **19**

7. a. On Saturday.

   b. They found a nice house downtown.

   c. Yes, they were.

8. a. I'm not sure.

   b. A small one.

   c. Sure, that's fine.

9. a. Apple juice, please.

   b. Yes, you can.

   c. OK. That sounds good.

10. a. About $250.

    b. No, it's not.

    c. It's dark blue.

PUT IT TOGETHER

Are You Green?

You can find many different types of surveys in magazines or on the Internet. Sometimes these surveys help you understand yourself and the way you think. Of course, they are not always correct!

You will hear a conversation about a survey that helps people learn how "green" they are—how often they do things that are good for the earth and the environment. How green are you?

■ **EXERCISE 1**

A. Vocabulary Preview *Study the words and their definitions. Then use the words to complete the sentences below.*

recycle: to use paper and other waste materials again for another purpose

electricity: energy used to make lights, computers, and other machines work

survey: a set of questions you ask people to find out about their behavior or opinions

cloth: material used for making clothes

throw away: get rid of things you do not want or need

turn off: make a machine stop working by stopping the power

1. I'm trying to make a phone call. Can you please _____ the television?

2. Don't _____ that old shirt! It's one of my favorites.

3. In the future, perhaps most people will drive _____ cars.

4. Put your old newspapers, cans, and bottles over there. The university will _____ them.

5. The man on the telephone was doing a _____. He asked me a lot of questions about the kinds of foods I buy.

6. That's a nice dress. I like the color, and the _____ is very soft.

B. 🎧 *Listen to the conversation. Check the survey questions that you hear.*

1. ☐ Do you take your own cloth bags to the supermarket?
2. ☐ Do you have a car?
3. ☐ Do you usually read the news in a newspaper or online?
4. ☐ Do you recycle old newspapers?
5. ☐ Is your home large or small?
6. ☐ Do you usually drive or walk to work?
7. ☐ Does your car use electricity?
8. ☐ When you leave a room, do you always turn off lights?
9. ☐ Is your computer's power on or off right now?
10. ☐ Are you interested in learning about more ways to be green?

C. 🎧 *Listen again. Use complete sentences to answer the questions.*

1. Is the survey in a magazine or online?

   _____

2. Does the woman think she is "green"?

   _____

3. Did the man want to take the survey?

   _____

4. Does the man take cloth bags to the supermarket?

   _____

5. Does the man read the news in the newspaper or online?

   _____

6. Does the man drive or walk to work?

   _____

7. Does the man's car use electricity?

   _____

8. Is the man's computer on or off?

   _____

■ **EXERCISE 2**

Work in groups. Compare your answers from Exercise 1C. Then ask and answer the questions in Exercise 1B. Who is the greenest person in the group?

UNIT 3 Understanding Contractions

Unit Warm Up

A. 🎧 *Talk about the picture with a partner. What are people doing? What do the signs mean? Listen and number the signs from 1–5.*

B. 🎧 *Listen again. Complete the park rules.*

1. You _____ swim here.

2. Please _____ on the grass.

3. Fires _____ allowed here.

4. _____ no fishing here.

5. Please _____ litter. You're making a mess.

SKILL PRESENTATION

When we speak or write in English, we often use *contractions*. A *contraction* is a short way to say or write two words together. To make a contraction, we leave out some letters and add an apostrophe (').

Examples

> *He is* = **He's**   *Do not* = **Don't**

Recognizing contractions when you hear them will help you understand natural English.

Personal Pronouns + *be* and *will*

We usually use contractions when we join personal pronouns (*I, you, he, she, it, we, they*) and auxiliary verbs (*be* and *will*).

Pronoun + *be*		Pronoun + *will*	
Full Form	**Contraction**	**Full Form**	**Contraction**
I am	**I'm**	I will	**I'll**
you are	**you're**	you will	**you'll**
he is / she is	**he's / she's**	he will / she will	**he'll / she'll**
it is	**it's**	it will	**it'll**
we are	**we're**	we will	**we'll**
they are	**they're**	they will	**they'll**

🎧 Listen and repeat.

1. He's a good friend of mine.
2. It'll take us an hour to get downtown.
3. She's going to wash her car this afternoon.
4. I'll have the chicken and rice, please.
5. Do you know what time they're leaving tomorrow?

☑ **Check Yourself**

A. 🎧 *Listen. Do you hear the full form or a contraction? Check (✓) the answer.*

	Full Form	Contraction
1.	☐	☐
2.	☐	☐
3.	☐	☐
4.	☐	☐
5.	☐	☐

> **Note**
> Sometimes speakers use the full form instead of the contraction for emphasis (to express strong feelings) or to disagree.
>
> **Examples**
> A: *I'm not going to clean my room.*
> B: *Yes, you are going to clean it, right now!*
>
> A: *Let's go out to eat tonight.*
> B: *OK. But we are not going to eat pizza again.*

B. 🎧 *Listen and write the contraction that you hear.*

1. _____ going to the store for some milk and bread.

2. _____ be the next class president.

3. I think _____ be here soon.

4. I heard _____ having a party this weekend.

5. Did you know _____ a singer?

6. _____ probably be sunny tomorrow.

7. Let's go eat. _____ hungry!

8. _____ going to pick you up at eight o'clock.

Negative Contractions

Another common type of contraction joins auxiliary verbs such as *be*, *do*, and *will* with the negative word *not*. We say and write the two words as one. To form a negative contraction, we leave out the letter *o* in the word *not*.

Examples

is not = isn't   *does not* = doesn't

be + not		do + not		will + not	
Full Form	**Contraction**	**Full Form**	**Contraction**	**Full Form**	**Contraction**
am not	----------	do not	**don't**	will not	**won't**
are not	**aren't**	does not	**doesn't**		
is not	**isn't**	did not	**didn't**		
was not	**wasn't**				
were not	**weren't**				

Note

There is no contraction for *am not*. Instead, we usually use the contraction *I'm* + *not*: *I'm not* tired.

The contraction for *will not* doesn't follow the typical pattern. The contraction is *won't*.

With personal pronouns + *be*, either of the following negative contractions are possible:

It's not my birthday today.   It isn't my birthday.
[pronoun + *be* contraction]   [*be* + *not* contraction]

🎧 Listen and repeat.

1. It isn't raining right now.
2. We don't understand this map.
3. It wasn't an expensive hotel.
4. She didn't see the stop sign.
5. He doesn't want to go shopping.
6. This won't happen again.

A. 🎧 *Listen. Do you hear the full form or a contraction? Check (✓) the answer.*

	Full Form	**Contraction**
1.	☐	☐
2.	☐	☐
3.	☐	☐
4.	☐	☐
5.	☐	☐
6.	☐	☐

B. 🎧 *Listen and write the contraction that you hear.*

1. It _____ very quiet in the library last night.

2. My car _____ use much gas.

3. Mark _____ a very good cook.

4. Minh _____ have much time.

5. They _____ have their umbrellas.

6. I _____ eat at that restaurant again.

Can and Can't

In English (especially U.S. English), it is often difficult to hear the difference between the words *can* and *can't*. One reason is that the letter *t* at the end of the word *can't* is not pronounced, or it is pronounced very lightly. Sometimes even native English speakers have problems hearing the difference.

Of course, it is often very important to hear these words clearly. If your friend tells you, "You can't use my car tonight" and you hear, "You can use my car tonight," you may have problems with your friend!

Read about the main differences between *can* and *can't*.

Vowel Sound

Can	**Can't**
The vowel *a* in *can* has a short, weak pronunciation. Some speakers pronounce it with the short *i* sound: /kɪn/. Some speakers don't pronounce the vowel at all, so the word sounds almost like /kn/.	The vowel sound in the word *can't*, /æ/, is longer and stronger than the vowel sound in *can*. It sounds like the vowel sound in the words *ant* or *dance*.

Sentence Stress

Can	Can't
The word *can* is usually unstressed in a sentence. It is not pronounced as strongly as the subject or the main verb.	The contraction *can't* (like most negative words) is usually stressed. It is pronounced as strongly as the main verb.
In the sentence, *I can ski*, we pronounce the words *I* and *ski* more strongly than *can*.	In the sentence, *I can't ski*, we stress both *can't* and *ski*.

🎧 *Listen and repeat.*

1. My friend can help you.
2. What can we do now?
3. She can sing very well.
4. I can't explain this very well.
5. He can't see well without his glasses.
6. I can't understand you.
7. You can use my car tonight.
8. That can't be true.

☑ Check Yourself

A. 🎧 *Listen. Do you hear* **can** *or* **can't**? *Check (✓) the answer.*

	can	can't
1.	☐	☐
2.	☐	☐
3.	☐	☐
4.	☐	☐
5.	☐	☐

B. 🎧 *Listen and write* **can** *or* **can't**.

1. You _____ sit here.
2. I _____ get up early in the morning.
3. _____ you wait a few minutes?
4. You _____ leave now.
5. Amy _____ play the guitar.
6. We _____ be there in a half hour.

Other Contractions

Other words can be contracted with auxiliary verbs. Here are some examples of other common contractions you will hear in spoken English. Many of these contractions are only used when speaking. They are not usually written in formal writing.

🎧 *Listen and repeat.*

Here/There + be	This/That + be or will	let's (let + us)
Here's your pizza. There're a lot of new students in the class.	That's the man who took my bag. This'll be easy. That'll be ok.	Let's have some dinner. Let's hurry.

Wh- words + be, will or did	Nouns + be or will
Do you know who's coming to dinner? Who'll drive me to the movies? What're those? When's Jennifer's birthday? Excuse me. Where's the library? Where'd you buy your computer? Why're they leaving? How're your sisters?	Jack's a friend of mine. These shoes're very nice Please be quiet. The baby'll wake up.

Note
We use the contraction *let's* to invite people to do things with us.
Let's can be used in formal writing.

🎧 *Listen. Use the correct contractions to complete the conversations.*

1. **A:** _____ the problem?

   B: My car _____ start.

2. **A:** _____ get a cup of coffee.

   B: _____ a great idea.

3. **A:** _____ you get that jacket?

   B: At Stewart's Department Store. _____ a big sale there this week.

4. **A:** The _____ waiting for you.

   B: Oh, no. I'm not ready. _____ my wallet?

5. **A:** _____ you going to get home tonight?

   B: _____ going to drive me.

6. **A:** _____ we do if it rains tomorrow?

   B: _____ go to the museum.

   A: Yeah. _____ be fun.

Contractions and Possessives

Possessive words (*my*, *your*, *his*, *her*, *our*) show who something belongs to. Some contractions sound just like possessives but they are spelled differently. You can tell whether a word is a contraction or a possession by listening to rest of the sentence.

Contraction	Possessive
you're (you + are) *You're* going to work now, right?	**your** (belongs to you) Are these *your* keys?
it's (it + is) *It's* time to feed the fish.	**its** (belongs to it) Did you give the fish *its* food?
they're (they + are) *They're* ready to go now.	**their** (belongs to them) *Their* room is ready.
Who's (who + is) *Who's* going swimming with me?	**Whose** *(belongs to whom)* *Whose* bicycle is this?

Contractions like *my brother's* and possessives like *my brother's* sound the same and are spelled the same.

Example

> *My brother's working right now.*
>
> *This is my brother's store.*

🎧 **Listen and repeat.**

1. You're a great singer.
2. The store changed its hours.
3. They're already late.
4. Is that your coffee cup?
5. It's a long walk to the train station from here.
6. Who's the star of this movie?
7. Their rent is going up next month.
8. Whose papers are these on the floor?
9. My sister's got a new job.

☑ **Check Yourself**

🎧 **Listen. Do you hear a contraction or a possessive form? Check (✓) the answer.**

	Contraction	Possessive
1.	☐	☐
2.	☐	☐
3.	☐	☐
4.	☐	☐
5.	☐	☐
6.	☐	☐
7.	☐	☐
8.	☐	☐
9.	☐	☐
10.	☐	☐

PRACTICE

■ **EXERCISE 1**

🎧 *Listen and write the contraction you hear. Then, circle each contraction in the puzzle. (Words can read from left to right, right to left, up to down, down to up, or diagonally.)*

1. _____Let's_____   8. _____

2. _____   9. _____

3. _____   10. _____

4. _____   11. _____

5. _____   12. _____

6. _____   13. _____

7. _____   14. _____

H	Z	S	L	X	D	C	M	P	H	T	H
W	W	S	'	E	R	E	H	W	Z	H	K
O	D	W	H	E	R	E	'	D	R	A	V
N	N	T	'	N	S	E	O	D	T	T	A
'	E	D	S	R	Q	G	G	'	C	'	I
T	R	G	'	S	E	H	N	V	M	S	A
A	'	S	T	W	C	S	S	H	E	'	S
U	Y	S	I	A	A	Z	Y	L	M	L	T
I	E	'	T	S	D	I	D	N	'	T	X
U	H	T	J	N	K	T	'	N	S	I	D
E	T	E	R	'	X	C	A	N	'	T	L
Z	N	L	U	T	H	O	W	'	S	D	B

🎧 *Informal greetings in English often begin with contractions. Listen and check (✓) the best response.*

1. a. ☐ Not much—how about with you?

    b. ☐ I don't know what went up.

2. a. ☐ To the library.

    b. ☐ Oh, pretty good.

3. a. ☐ Just great—you?

    b. ☐ I'm studying.

4. a. ☐ The bicycle is new.

    b. ☐ Well, I got a new job.

5. a. ☐ Not much, really.

    b. ☐ It already happened.

■ EXERCISE 3

🎧 *Listen and circle the correct contractions. Then practice the conversations with a partner.*

Conversation 1: Birthday party

A: So, *(what're / how're)* you doing this weekend?

B: I don't know yet. Why? *(What's / Who's)* going on?

A: *(I'm / We're)* planning to drive down to Westport.

B: Oh really? *(What're / Why're)* you going there?

A: My *(brother's / mother's)* going to college there.

B: Oh, I *(don't / didn't)* know that.

A: Yeah, and *(it's / isn't)* his birthday Saturday, so *(he's / we're)* having a party.

B: *(What'll / What're)* you getting him?

A: *(I'm / It's)* not sure. He loves music.

B: How about tickets to a concert?

A: I *(can't / don't)* afford that. It's expensive to go to concerts these days.

B: *(That's / That'll)* true. Well, maybe you can get him a CD.

Conversation 2: Ordering pizza

A: *(I'm / We're)* hungry.

B: *(We're / They're)* both hungry, too. *(Let's / We'll)* order some Chinese food.

C: I *(can't / don't)* feel like Chinese food tonight.

A: OK. *(I'll / We'll)* order a pizza then.

B: OK. *(What'll / What's)* we have on it?

C: Ummmm .... how about onions?

B: No, I *(can't / won't)* eat onions. How about mushrooms?

A: Mushrooms ... *(They're / That's)* a good idea. And sausage?

C: I *(don't / didn't)* eat sausage. *(It's / I'm)* a vegetarian.

B: Oh, right. One mushroom pizza. Small, medium, or large?

A: *(I'm / I'll)* pretty hungry. *(Let's / It's)* get a large one.

B: Fine. *(Who'll / Who's)* call Mario's?

C: *(I'll / He'll)* do it.

■ **EXERCISE 4**

Work with a partner. Correct any mistakes in these sentences. (Some sentences are correct).

1. Their leaving early in the morning.
2. Who's going to pick up Mr. Thomas at the airport?
3. Please move. Your standing on my foot.
4. Every state in the United States has it's own flag.
5. Who's test is this? It doesn't have a name on it.
6. It's almost midnight—time for me to go to bed!
7. You're car is parked behind mine—can you please move it?

■ **EXERCISE 5**

🎧 *Listen and write the questions. Then ask and answer the questions with a partner.*

1. _____
2. _____
3. _____

(continued)

4. _____

5. _____

6. _____

7. _____

8. _____

PUT IT TOGETHER

Proverbs

A *proverb* is a popular saying that many people from a culture know and use. Proverbs usually give some advice or teach an important lesson. Many proverbs use contractions. In this section, you will learn some common English proverbs and their meanings.

■ EXERCISE 1

A. Vocabulary Preview *Match each word to the correct definition.*

_____ 1. basket

_____ 2. trick

_____ 3. grow

_____ 4. mice

_____ 5. oil

_____ 6. mix

a. when living things get bigger

b. a skill

c. join together to form something new

d. a thick liquid made from vegetables, often used for frying (cooking) food

e. a container made of thin pieces of wood, used for holding things

f. (plural of *mouse*) small animals with long tails that sometimes live in people's houses

B. 🎧 *Listen and complete the proverbs.*

1. _____ no place like _____.

2. Money _____ _____ on trees.

3. When the _____ away, the _____ play.

4. _____ and water _____ mix.

5. You _____ teach an old dog new _____.

6. _____ put all your eggs in one _____.

C. Write the number of each proverb from Exercise B next to its meaning. Then compare your answers with a partner.

_____ 1. It's difficult to learn new things when you are older.

_____ 2. Home is the best place to be.

_____ 3. People who are very different can't get along.

_____ 4. People have to work hard to make money.

_____ 5. When no one is watching, people will do as they like.

_____ 6. Don't choose only one thing; try to have many choices.

■ EXERCISE 2

A. Work in a group. Think of three proverbs from your culture. How can you say them in English? What do they mean?

Proverb	Meaning

B. Join another group. Share your proverbs from Exercise A.

Unit Warm Up

Look at the photos with a partner. How many numbers can you find?
How do you say them in English?

SKILL PRESENTATION

Even though you may know numbers in English, it's sometimes difficult to understand them, especially when someone speaks quickly or gives a lot of numbers at one time. When you listen in English, you may need to listen for many different types of numbers; for example, telephone numbers, addresses, times of day, or prices. It is also important to hear numbers correctly when you listen to a lecture, attend a meeting, or talk on the telephone.

Numbers 1–100

🎧 *Listen and repeat.*

1	one	11	eleven	30	thirty
2	two	12	twelve	40	forty
3	three	13	thirteen	50	fifty
4	four	14	fourteen	60	sixty
5	five	15	fifteen	70	seventy
6	six	16	sixteen	80	eighty
7	seven	17	seventeen	90	ninety
8	eight	18	eighteen	100	one (a) hundred
9	nine	19	nineteen		
10	ten	20	twenty		

☑ **Check Yourself**

🎧 *Listen and write the missing numbers.*

1. The bank is at _____72_____ Union Street.
2. The store opens at _____8:30_____ A.M.
3. My sister will be _____24_____ years old next week.
4. There are over _____100_____ students at this school.
5. His family moved here in _____1997_____.
6. We live about _____2.5_____ kilometers from here.
7. Our flight leaves in about _____45_____ minutes.
8. The golf course is at the corner of Highway _____6_____ and Route _____39_____.
9. My cell phone number is _____802 555 0250_____.

Numbers Ending in -*teen* and -*ty*

Two kinds of numbers are especially hard to understand:

Numbers that end in -*teen* can be pronounced in two ways: with the stress on the second syllable, or with equal stress on the first and second syllables.

Examples

(13) thir **teen** or **thir teen**

(15) fif **teen** or **fif teen**

(19) nine **teen** or **nine teen**

When you say numbers that end in -*ty*, the stress is on the first part of the word. In other words, the first part of the word is a little stronger and louder.

Examples

(30) **thir** ty   (50) **fif** ty   (90) **nine** ty

> **Note**
> - The number *0* is sometimes pronounced like the letter *O*; for example, in phone numbers and addresses: 305 Main Street = *three oh five Main Street*.
> - In numbers, the decimal point symbol (.) is pronounced *point*.

🎧 *Listen and repeat.*

Numbers ending in -**teen**

thir **teen**	or	**thir teen**
four **teen**	or	**four teen**
fif **teen**	or	**fif teen**
six **teen**	or	**six teen**
seven **teen**	or	**seven teen**
eight **teen**	or	**eight teen**
nine **teen**	or	**nine teen**

Numbers ending in -**ty**

twen ty	**seven** ty
thir ty	**eigh** ty
for ty	**nine** ty
fif ty	
six ty	

🎧 *Listen. Circle the correct numbers to complete the conversation.*

1.

Woman: Oh, you live in Mapleton Apartments, too? Which apartment do you live in?

Man: I live in number (*19 / 90*), on the east side. How about you?

Woman: We're in apartment (*14 / 40*), on the top floor.

2.

Man: How old were Aunt Maude and Uncle Paul when they got married?

Woman: Let's see...I think she was (*16 / 60*) and he was (*17 / 70*).

Man: That's a little unusual, isn't it?

3.

Woman: So who won the game?

Man: Our team won by (*15 / 50*) points.

Woman: You must have some good players this year.

Man: Yeah, John McNeil scored (*13 / 30*) points himself.

4.

Woman: How are you doing with that crossword puzzle?

Man: Pretty well—I've finished all but (*18 / 80*) down and (*14 / 40*) across.

Woman: Do you want some help? I'm pretty good at crossword puzzles.

5.

Woman: I thought you said the hotel was only a (*15 / 50*) meter walk from the beach.

Man: No, you misunderstood me. I said it was a (*15 / 50*) *minute* walk.

6.

Woman: I need another (*19 / 90*) cents to buy this magazine. Can you lend it to me?

Man: Let me see how much change I have...Umm, no, sorry. I only have (*15 / 50*) cents.

Letters

It is also important to understand letters when you listen. If you don't understand a word or a name, you might ask someone to spell it for you. Or you may need to hear letters correctly when you listen to abbreviations (such as *U.K.* for United Kingdom or *ATM* for Automated Teller Machine), passwords, reservation numbers, and so on.

Some letters may be harder to understand than others because they sound like other letters. Or it may be difficult for you because, in your own language, the letter sounds may be different from the letter sound in English. For example, the three vowels *A*, *I*, and *E* are difficult for many learners because they have similar sounds in other languages.

Below are some examples of letters that can be difficult for some English learners.

🎧 *Listen and repeat.*

Vowels

A (as in **a**pple)　　**I** (as in **i**ce cream)　　**E** (as in **e**lephant)

Consonants

B (as in **b**aby)　　**P** (as in **P**eter)　　**V** (as in **v**ictory)

G (as in **g**as)　　**J** (as in **j**ump)

S (as in **S**am)　　**F** (as in **f**ather)

M (as in **m**other)　　**N** (as in **n**oodle)

> **Note**
> In the U.S., the letter *Z* is usually pronounced *zee*. In the U.K. and most other English-speaking countries (Australia, New Zealand, Canada, South Africa, and so on), this letter is usually pronounced *zed*: *zee as in zebra* or *zed as in zebra*.

☑ Check Yourself

🎧 *Listen and circle the correct answer.*

1. The woman's last name is _____.
   a. Peirce
   b. Bierce
   c. Price

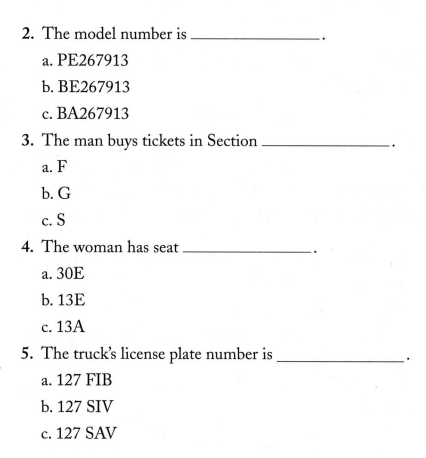

2. The model number is _____.

    a. PE267913

    b. BE267913

    c. BA267913

3. The man buys tickets in Section _____.

    a. F

    b. G

    c. S

4. The woman has seat _____.

    a. 30E

    b. 13E

    c. 13A

5. The truck's license plate number is _____.

    a. 127 FIB

    b. 127 SIV

    c. 127 SAV

PRACTICE

■ EXERCISE 1

🎧 *Listen to the conversations. Use numbers to complete the sentences.*

1.

Man:	I heard you're flying to Singapore next week.
Woman:	Yeah, it's a non-stop flight. It takes nearly _____ hours.
Man:	Wow, that's a long time.
Woman:	The last time I went to Singapore, the flight stopped in Frankfurt, Germany for _____ hours. The trip took nearly _____ hours.
Man:	But you'd rather fly non-stop wouldn't you?
Woman:	I guess so. But that's a long time to sit on a plane without a break. And I'll only be in Singapore for _____ days.
Man:	Wow, in less than one week, you'll spend _____ hours in the air.

(continued)

2.

Man: My brother was in a triathlon last weekend.

Woman: What's a triathlon?

Man: It's a ____ part race. First, you have to swim for ____ kilometers.

Woman: Uh-huh.

Man: Then you ride a bicycle for ____ kilometers. And after that you have to run for ____ kilometers.

Woman: Wow! Your brother must be in really good shape! How long did it take him?

Man: It took him almost ____ hours. But he was happy just to finish.

Woman: Yeah, I can understand why!

3.

Man: Good morning. This is Frank Williams. I'd like to make an appointment to see Doctor Martinez.

Woman: Yes, Mr. Williams. Can I have your home phone number?

Man: Sure. It's _____.

Woman: Is that area code _____?

Man: No, it's _____.

Woman: And your home address?

Man: I live at ____ East Willow Road, apartment ____ in Cambridge.

Woman: Zip code?

Man: It's _____.

Woman: I have an appointment available ____ weeks from today at ____ o'clock.

Man: OK. That'll be fine.

Note
- An area code is the number before a local phone number that indicates a city or area.
- A zip code is a postal code used in the U.S. to indicate a specific town, city, or part of a city.

4.

Woman: The Euro is used in ＿＿ of the ＿＿ countries of the European Union. There are ＿＿ Eurocents in a Euro. For paper bills, there are ＿＿ Euro, ＿＿ Euro, ＿＿ Euro, ＿＿ Euro, and ＿＿ Euro banknotes. What about coins? There are ＿＿ and ＿＿ Euro coins, and ＿＿, ＿＿. ＿＿, and ＿＿ Eurocent coins. In some countries, you will also see ＿＿ and ＿＿ Eurocent coins.

■ EXERCISE 2

🎧 *Listen. When the speaker spells a word or uses an abbreviation (such as UN for United Nations) write the letters you hear. There is one letter for each blank.*

1.

    a. ＿＿ ＿＿ ＿＿ ＿＿   ＿＿ ＿＿ ＿＿ ＿＿

    b. ＿＿ ＿＿ ＿＿ ＿＿   ＿＿ ＿＿ ＿＿ ＿＿ ＿＿ ＿＿

2.

    a. ＿＿ ＿＿ ＿＿ ＿＿

    b. ＿＿ ＿＿ ＿＿

    c. ＿＿ ＿＿ ＿＿ ＿＿ ＿＿ ＿＿ ＿＿ ＿＿

3.

    a. ＿＿ ＿＿ ＿＿

    b. ＿＿ ＿＿ ＿＿

    c. ＿＿ ＿＿ ＿＿

    d. ＿＿ ＿＿

    e. ＿＿ ＿＿

4.

    a. ＿＿ ＿＿

    b. ＿＿ ＿＿

    c. ＿＿ ＿＿ ＿＿

    d. ＿＿ ＿＿ ＿＿

    e. ＿＿ ＿＿

5.

    a. ＿＿ ＿＿ ＿＿ ＿＿

    b. ＿＿ ＿＿ ＿＿ ＿＿

    c. ＿＿ ＿＿

    d. ＿＿ ＿＿ ＿＿

    e. ＿＿ ＿＿ ＿＿

■ EXERCISE 3

🎧 *Listen and write the missing numbers and letters.*

1.
TR __ 6 __ H __ 9 __

2.

AIRLINE BOARDING PASS

NAME OF PASSENGER
Maria Garcia

FROM LGA

TO DFW

CARRIER	FLIGHT	CLASS	DATE	TIME
TWA	17	Coach	9/4/10	3:10PM

RESERVATION NUMBER
VY____-2____76-____

GATE	BOARDING TIME	SEAT
27	**245P**	**12A**

3.

Log in

User Name:

Password:

4.

TO:

Natalie _____

_____ Hill Street

West _____, Australia

Postal Code _____

5.

Great Buy Computers

💻 **GREAT BUY COMPUTERS - Order Form**

Item: Laptop case - _____ inches

Sale price: $ _____

Credit card number: _____

Name: _____

PUT IT TOGETHER

Important Telephone Numbers

What telephone number do you call in your country if there is an accident, fire, or if you need the police? These numbers are different, depending on where you are in the world. Before you travel to another country, it's always a good idea to learn these telephone numbers. That way you'll be able to get help quickly if you have a problem.

A. Vocabulary Preview *Study the words and their definitions. Then use the words to complete the sentences below.*

emergency: a very serious or dangerous situation

operator: a person who connects telephone calls

system: a way of doing something

ambulance: a special vehicle for driving hurt or sick people to the hospital

report: to tell someone about something that happened

convenient: useful and easy to use

1. If you see this man, please call the police and _____ it right away.

2. I need to make an international call, but I'm not sure how. Do you think the _____ will help me?

3. We put all my computer files online, so we won't lose anything. It's a really good _____ .

4. Email is very _____ . It makes communication fast and easy.

5. The alarm will sound if there is an _____ , such as a fire.

6. He wasn't hurt very badly, but he still went to the hospital in an _____ .

B. 🎧 *Listen. Then read the statements and check (✓) true or false.*

	True	False
1. One hundred years ago, people usually called the operator for emergencies.	☐	☐
2. The first emergency number started in London on June 13, 1937.	☐	☐
3. The number 911 was first used in the U.K.	☐	☐
4. Canada and the U.S. have the same emergency number.	☐	☐
5. In Brazil, there are two different emergency numbers.	☐	☐
6. You can call 112 for an emergency from most cell phones.	☐	☐

C. 🎧 *Listen to an excerpt from the talk and complete the chart.*

Country	Emergency Numbers
Canada / U.S.A.	
New Zealand	
Australia	
U.K.	
Brazil	Police: Ambulance: Fire:
Korea	Police: Fire/ Ambulance: Report a spy:
European Union	

■ **EXERCISE 2**

A. *In the box below, write five numbers that are important in your life. For example, you can write numbers from your address, your age, a family member's birthday, the bus number you take to school, your best friend's birthday, the first few numbers of your cell phone number, etc.*

B. *Work in groups. Guess what each person's numbers are.*

Example

     A: Is 17 your age?

     B: No, guess again.

     A: Is it part of your address?

     B: Yes, it's my apartment number.

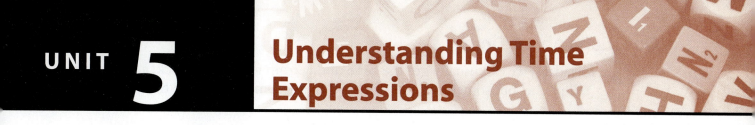

UNIT **5**

Understanding Time Expressions

Unit Warm Up

A. *Work with a partner. Talk about ways to say these times.*

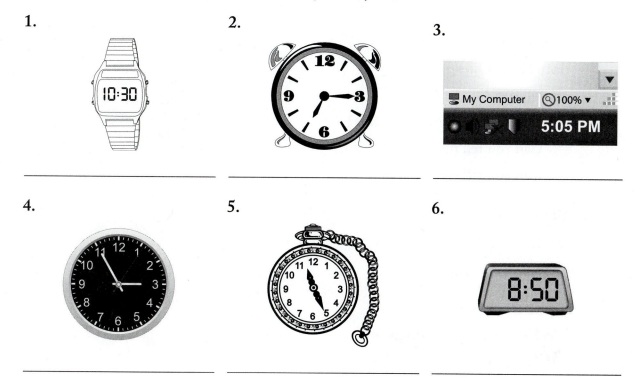

1.

2.

3.

4.

5.

6.

B. 🎧 *Listen and write the time below each picture.*

SKILL PRESENTATION

Time is an important part of our lives. Everyone needs to understand time expressions and be able to talk about time. In English, we often use different expressions to talk about the same time.

Example

10:30 may be said as ten-thirty *or* half past ten.

It's helpful to learn the different ways of talking about time so you can understand them when you hear them.

Questions About Time

Nowadays, we can usually get the time of day from a watch, a clock, a computer, or a cell phone, but sometimes, we still need to ask someone for the time.

Asking For the Time

🎧 *Listen and repeat.*

Direct Questions

What time is it?

Do you have the time?

More Polite Questions

Excuse me...

Do you know what time it is?

Can you tell me what time it is?

Can you tell me the time, please?

> **Note**
> To get someone's attention before asking for the time, people often begin with *Excuse me....*

Asking About the Time of Events

People may also ask what time an event starts or ends.

🎧 *Listen and repeat.*

Direct Questions

When does the meeting start?

What time does the meeting start?

More Polite Questions

Excuse me...

Do you know when the meeting starts?

Can you tell me what time the meeting starts?

Do you know what time the meeting starts?

Telling Time

The Exact Hour

The expression "o'clock" is often used to express time at the exact hour, but speakers may use other expressions, too.

🎧 *Listen and repeat.*

It's …

two o'clock.

two.

two A.M. *(in the morning)*

two P.M. *(in the afternoon)*

two sharp. *(exactly at two)*

The 12:00 Hour

There are several expressions for the time 12:00, depending on whether it is night or day.

🎧 *Listen and repeat.*

It's …

twelve.

midnight.

twelve midnight.

It's …

twelve.

noon.

midday.

twelve noon.

Hour and Minutes

One easy way to tell time is to use two numbers—one for the hour and one for the minutes. These two numbers are read separately. This way of telling time is common when reading digital watches or clocks.

Example

7:25 Seven twenty-five   **11:40 Eleven forty**

🎧 *Listen and repeat.*

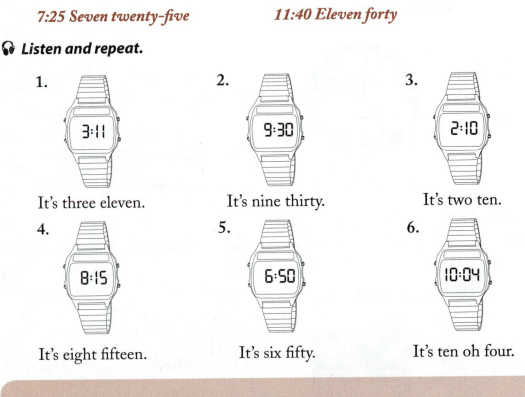

1. It's three eleven.

2. It's nine thirty.

3. It's two ten.

4. It's eight fifteen.

5. It's six fifty.

6. It's ten oh four.

Note
For times between 01 and 09 minutes after the hour, zero is pronounced *oh*—like the letter O.

☑ **Check Yourself**

🎧 *Listen and write the two times in each sentence.*

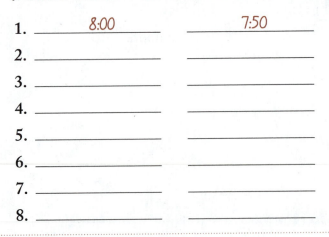

1. _____8:00_____   _____7:50_____
2. _____   _____
3. _____   _____
4. _____   _____
5. _____   _____
6. _____   _____
7. _____   _____
8. _____   _____

Time After the Hour

The words *after* or *past* can also be used to talk about times after the hour.

For 15 minutes after the hour, we use the expressions *quarter past* or *quarter after*.

For 30 minutes after, we can say, for example, *thirty* or *half past*.

> **Note**
> We <u>only</u> use *after* or *past* with times between 01 and 29 minutes past the hour and only with five minute periods, for example, *five after two, ten past four, twenty-five after eight*. It is NOT common to hear these expressions with other times, for example, *two after eleven* or *twenty-three past five*.

🎧 *Listen and repeat.*

1.

It's five past ten.

2.

It's twenty after seven.

3.

It's ten past six.

4.

It's eight fifteen.

It's quarter after eight.

It's quarter past eight.

5.

It's one thirty.

It's half past one.

Time Before the Hour

We use the prepositions *of, to,* or *till* when we talk about times before the hour.

For fifteen minutes before the hour, we say *quarter of* or *quarter to.*

🎧 *Listen and repeat.*

1.

It's ten to nine.

2.

It's twenty of seven.

3.

It's five till twelve.

4.

It's three forty-five.

It's quarter to four.

It's quarter of four.

It's quarter till four.

☑ **Check Yourself**

Write two different ways to express each time.

1. 2:00

   It's two o'clock.

   It's two.

2. 5:45

   _____

   _____

3. 9:15

   _____

   _____

4. 12:00

_____

_____

5. 6:50

_____

_____

6. 10:25

_____

_____

7. 12:30

_____

_____

8. 1:55

_____

_____

Note

When it is clear from the conversation what hour the speaker is talking about, the speaker may not say the hour. For example, in the conversation below, it's clear the man means quarter after nine.

Woman: "Why don't we meet at nine?"

Man: "How about quarter after?"

PRACTICE

■ EXERCISE 1

🎧 *Listen to each conversation. Then read the question and mark the time on the clock. The first one is done as an example.*

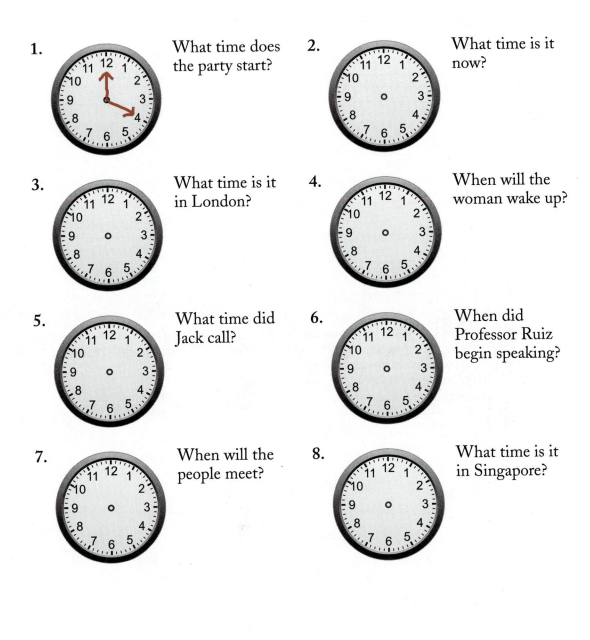

1. What time does the party start?

2. What time is it now?

3. What time is it in London?

4. When will the woman wake up?

5. What time did Jack call?

6. When did Professor Ruiz begin speaking?

7. When will the people meet?

8. What time is it in Singapore?

■ EXERCISE 2

The United States has six different time zones: Eastern, Central, Mountain, Pacific, Alaskan, and Hawaiian. As you move from east to west, the time of day becomes *earlier*, so when it is 2:00 P.M. in the Eastern time zone, it is 1:00 P.M. Central time, noon Mountain time, and 11 A.M. Pacific.

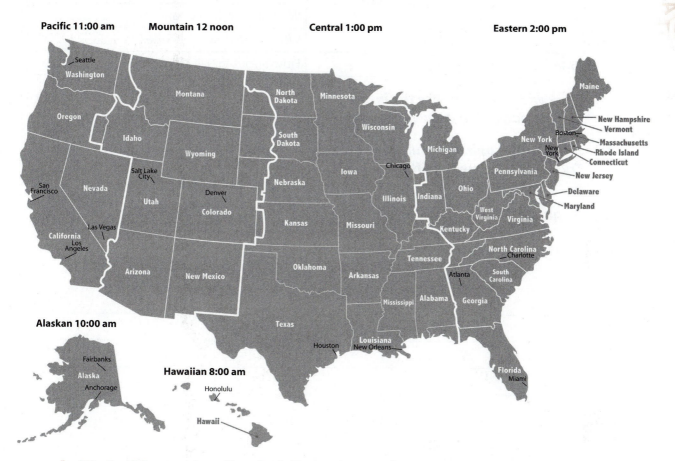

A. Work with a partner. Use the information on the map to complete the chart.

City	Time Zone	Time
New York	*Eastern*	*9:00 P.M.*
Chicago		
Denver		
San Francisco		
Anchorage		
Honolulu		

B.  *Listen and use numbers to write the times in the first column only.*

1. It's _____ in Boston right now.	What time is it in Houston? _____
2. It's _____ in Los Angeles.	What's the time in Atlanta? _____
3. Right now in Las Vegas, it's _____.	What about in Minneapolis? _____
4. It's _____ in Honolulu.	What time is it in Charlotte? _____
5. It's _____ in Miami.	What's the time in Seattle? _____
6. In New Orleans, it's _____.	How about in Salt Lake City? _____

C. *Work with a partner. Use the information in the first column of Exercise B and the map on page 57 to answer the questions in the second column.*

D. *Join another pair. Take turns asking and answering the questions from Exercise B. Try to say the times in different ways.*

■ EXERCISE 3

A. *Listen and answer the questions with complete sentences.*

1. _____
2. _____
3. _____
4. _____
5. _____
6. _____
7. _____
8. _____

B. *Work with a partner. Share your answers from Exercise A. Write your partner's answers.*

1. _____
2. _____
3. _____
4. _____
5. _____
6. _____
7. _____
8. _____

PUT IT TOGETHER

■ **EXERCISE 1**

The Canadian

Built in the 1800s, the Trans-Canadian Railroad stretches over 6,000 kilometers, from Canada's east coast to its west coast. One of the most popular trips on the Trans-Canadian Railroad is aboard a train called *The Canadian*. This train leaves from Toronto and then travels across the plains and through the beautiful mountains of western Canada. After a five-day trip, it arrives in Vancouver on the Pacific Coast.

A. Vocabulary Preview *Read each sentence. Then circle the best definition for the underlined word.*

1. You will <u>board</u> *The Canadian* at Union Station in Toronto.

   a. travel   b. get on   c. look for

2. On day one of our trip, the train <u>departs</u> from Toronto.

   a. stops   b. flies   c. leaves

3. The <u>scenery</u> on this part of the trip is especially beautiful.

   a. train   b. views   c. food

4. On day five, you arrive at your final <u>destination</u>.

   a. place you are traveling to   b. place where you live   c. place where you work

B. *Listen and draw the route of* The Canadian *on the map.*

C. 🎧 *Listen again and write the times in the schedule. Then check your answers with a partner.*

Trans-Canadian Railway

Toronto–Vancouver   *The Canadian*

	DESTINATION	SCHEDULE
Day 1:	Toronto	Departs: _____
Day 3:	Winnipeg	Arrives: _____
		Departs: _____
	Saskatoon	Arrives: _____
		Departs: _____
Day 4:	Edmonton	Arrives: _____
		Departs: _____
	Jasper	Arrives: _____
		Departs: _____
	Kamloops	Arrives: _____
		Departs: _____
Day 5:	Vancouver	Arrives: _____

■ EXERCISE 2

Ask your classmates questions to complete the survey. When a classmate answers yes, write his or her name in the chart. Then ask the time and write it.

Example

> *A: Did you wake up very early today?*
>
> *B: Yes, I did.*
>
> *A: What time did you wake up?*
>
> *B: At quarter past six.*

Find someone who ...	Classmate	Time
woke up very early today.		
stayed up late last night.		
usually sleeps late on weekends.		
works in the evening.		
can tell you the time right now.		
has a class early in the morning.		
usually eats dinner at the same time as you.		
will get home earlier than you today.		

Comprehension Focus

Unit Warm Up

Work with a partner. Look at the pictures and discuss the questions.

- Where are these places? What's happening?
- What are the people probably talking about? What do you think they are saying?
- What kinds of things are the people listening to? Why are they listening?

SKILL PRESENTATION

Every day, we listen to many types of information and for many different reasons. Sometimes, when listening in English, you may feel worried or nervous when you miss some words or information. But even if you don't understand everything that is said, it is still possible to understand what's important.

It's important to remember why you are listening.

Main Ideas

The *main idea* is the general topic or subject of the conversation. In a longer talk, the main idea is the most important one. For example, if you hear your teacher talking, it's important to know if he or she is talking about the homework, teaching a new grammar point, or just chatting about the weekend.

Here are some examples of main ideas:
- The speakers are talking about a sports event.
- A teacher is making an announcement about a test.
- The radio ad is about a sale in a department store.

Knowing the main idea helps you know
- if the talk is important,
- what kind of vocabulary and ideas you might hear,
- if you should also pay attention to details.

When you listen for main ideas, ask yourself:
- What is this conversation or talk about?
- What are the most important points or ideas?

Listen for *key words*. These words can tell you the main idea even if you don't catch many details. For example, if you are listening to a radio report, and the announcer is speaking very fast, but you catch only the words *baseball*, *team*, and *championship game*, then you know you are listening to a program about sports and not a news program or a weather report.

☑ Check Yourself

A. 🎧 *Listen and circle the correct answer.*

1. What is this talk about?

   a. It's advertising cars for sale.

   b. It's celebrating the season of spring.

   c. It's talking about ways to save time.

2. Who are the speakers?

   a. a police officer and someone who needs help

   b. a store clerk and a customer

   c. a husband and wife

3. Where would you hear this announcement?

   a. in an airport

   b. in a store

   c. on the radio

B. 🎧 *Work with a partner. Listen again. Talk about which key words helped you find the right answers.*

Details

Details are specific pieces of information, for example, a person's name, a price, where to meet someone, or a time.

Imagine that you call a movie theater to find out the time of a movie you want to see. What information do you need to listen for? Just the name and time of the movie. If you understand everything else but miss those details, your listening is not successful. But if you only understand those details and nothing else, your listening is successful.

When you listen for details, ask yourself:
- What do I really need to know?
- What will that information sound like? That is, what kinds of vocabulary words do I expect?

☑ Check Yourself

A. 🎧 *Listen. You will hear a conversation in a restaurant. First read the questions and think about what words and phrases you might hear in the conversation. Then listen and write the answers to the questions.*

1. What does the man want to order for lunch? _____

2. What does the woman want to drink? _____

3. How much does the chocolate cake cost? _____

B. *Work with a partner. Write* **M** *if the information is a main idea or* **D** *if the information is a detail.*

   D   1. a person's home address

_____ 2. the subject of the talk is "Alaska"

_____ 3. two people are talking about a news story they heard

_____ 4. the total price of the camera

_____ 5. your teacher's email address

_____ 6. what time the store closes

_____ 7. the next train will be late

_____ 8. your friend's cell phone number

_____ 9. what color uniform you will have to buy

_____ 10. some people are talking about where they work

C. *Check your answers with another pair. For the details in Exercise B, talk about some words or phrases you might hear. Then share them with the class.*

Example
....

> *For a person's home address, you might hear numbers, a city name, and the words* **street** *or* **apartment**.

PRACTICE

In these exercises, you will hear each recording twice. The first time, listen for the main ideas. Then listen again for details.

■ EXERCISE 1

A. 🎧 **Main Ideas** *Listen. Circle the correct answer to complete each statement.*

1. The speaker is _____.

   a. at a restaurant.

   b. at the bank.

   c. in a classroom.

2. The speaker is a ___.

   a. waiter

   b. teacher

   c. student

3. The purpose of the talk is to ___.

   a. explain a mistake

   b. ask for help

   c. tell people to do something

> **Tip**
> Before you listen, look at any pictures and read the exercises. Then you will know more about what to listen for. This strategy is especially useful on listening tests!

B. 🎧 **Details** *Listen again. Circle the correct word to complete the sentence.*

1. (*Monday / Tuesday*) is a holiday.

2. Students should use the (*textbook / workbook*).

3. The assignment is on page (*23 / 32*).

4. The last problem is number (*41 / 49*).

5. The (*information is / answers are*) in the back of the book.

6. Students should check their answers (*before / during*) the next class.

■ EXERCISE 2

A. 🎧 **Main Ideas** *Listen and circle the correct answer.*

1. Who are the speakers?

   a. They're friends.

   b. They're family members.

   c. They don't know each other.

2. What are they talking about?

   a. ordering food

   b. why the woman is late

   c. problems with the woman's car

3. What are they going to do next?

   a. go to a coffee shop

   b. go home

   c. go to class

B. *Work with a partner. Talk about which key words helped you find the right answers.*

C. 🎧 **Details** *Listen again. Check (✓) the problems the woman mentions.*

☐ She couldn't find her keys.

☐ Her mother called her.

☐ Her car wouldn't start.

☐ She forgot the CDs.

☐ She lost her way.

☐ The traffic was bad.

☐ She couldn't find a place to park.

☐ She had to return a book to the library.

☐ She stopped to buy coffee.

☐ She had to walk a long way.

■ EXERCISE 3

A. 🎧 **Main Ideas** *Listen and write **T** for True or **F** for False.*

_____ 1. The speakers are in a store.

_____ 2. The man's camera doesn't work.

_____ 3. The man needs to find his receipt.

_____ 4. The man needs to take the camera back to the store.

_____ 5. The woman knows what the problem with the camera is.

B. 🎧 **Details** *Listen again. Cross out any incorrect information and write the correct information above it.*

1. He bought the camera two years ago.

2. He can't print pictures.

3. He bought the camera in June.

4. He needs to mail the camera to the sales center.

5. The man was taking pictures in the mountains.

■ EXERCISE 4

A. Vocabulary Preview *Study the words and their definitions. Then use the words to complete the sentences below.*

hunt:	look for food
diet:	the kinds of food you eat
unfortunately:	sadly
store:	keep for a period of time
survive:	stay alive

1. I wanted to go dancing last Friday, but _____ , I got sick.

2. John's doctor said he should change his _____ and lose some weight.

3. You should _____ your camera in a safe place.

4. Many animals _____ at night. It's easier to catch their food in the dark.

5. How long can a person _____ without food and water?

B. 🎧 Main Ideas *Listen. What is the main idea? Number the pictures in order from 1 to 5. (There is one extra.)*

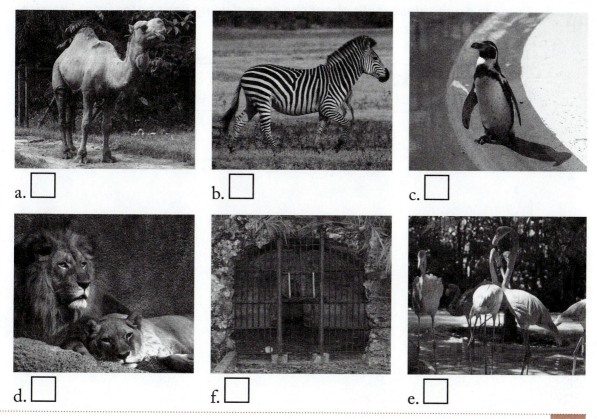

a. ☐   b. ☐   c. ☐

d. ☐   f. ☐   e. ☐

C. **Details** *Listen again. Circle the correct word to complete the sentence.*

1. In the zoo, lions (*eat / sleep*) a lot.
2. Flamingos get their (*color / size*) from what they eat.
3. The elephants will be back in about (*15 days / a month*).
4. The humps on their backs contain (*water / fat*).
5. Penguins spend about (*25% / 50%*) of their lives on land.

■ EXERCISE 5

A. *Think of an animal you know about. It could be a wild animal or one you have as a pet. Write details about each of these main ideas.*

Main Ideas	Details
Appearance	
What It Eats / What It Does	
Where It's From / Where It Lives	
Interesting Facts	

B. *Prepare a one-minute talk about the animal using your notes from Exercise A. Then give the talk to a partner.*

> **Applying Your Skills** For additional practice in listening for main ideas and details, turn to Part 2, Unit 3, pages 79–82 and Unit 4, pages 83–88.

Unit Warm Up

Work with a partner. Look at the pictures and discuss the questions.

- What do you think the people in the pictures are saying?
- How do you think they are feeling? Why do you think so?

SKILL PRESENTATION

To *infer* or *make an inference* means to decide that something is probably true based on what you see or hear. For example, in the Unit Warm Up, you inferred the speakers' feelings from the situations in the pictures.

We often make inferences about the following types of information:

- the topic of the conversation or talk (what the speakers are talking about)

- background information about the speakers and situation (who the speakers are, what is happening)

- the speakers' relationship (friends, co-workers, people who don't know each other)

- the speakers' attitudes (their ideas and feelings about the topic)

- what will happen next (Will the speakers meet later? What the speaker will decide to do about a problem.)

When you listen in English, you can use inference skills to help you understand more information.

☑ Check Yourself

🎧 *Listen and circle the correct answer.*

1. You might hear this announcement _____.

   a. at a restaurant or theater

   b. on a radio program

2. The speakers _____.

   a. know each other

   b. don't know each other

3. The speakers probably _____ play soccer.

   a. will

   b. won't

4. The women are _____.

   a. pleased

   b. unhappy

Indirect Language

Speakers don't always say what they are thinking. There can be different reasons for this. They might not want to sound rude or to hurt a listener's feelings. They might feel embarrassed or shy.

When a speaker doesn't state his or her feelings directly, you may have to *infer*, or guess, the true meaning. For example, you probably learned while studying English grammar that the answer to a question such as, *Do you want to go to a movie with me?*, will be *Yes, I do* or *No, I don't*.

However, English speakers might answer like this:

For Yes: *I'd love a chance to do something fun this weekend!*

For No: *I'm really tired tonight. And I have to get up early tomorrow.*

If you are waiting to hear a yes or a no, you might miss the speaker's answer. However, if you pay attention to what the speaker is saying and the speaker's tone of voice, you can usually figure out if the speaker really means yes or no.

☑ Check Yourself

A. 🎧 *Listen. For the questions at the left, write Y by the answers that mean "yes" and N by the answers that mean "no."*

B. 🎧 *Listen again. Circle the answers to the questions at the right.*

1. Do you want to study for the test together?

    _____ a. I'm pretty busy this weekend.

    _____ b. I'm so lost in that class. I need all the help I can get!

    _____ c. I always study better with a friend.

    _____ d. I'm probably not going to study for that test.

    Who are the speakers?

    a. classmates

    b. strangers

    c. a parent and child

    d. a teacher and student

2. Didn't you just love the new Space Wars movie?

    _____ a. I'm not really into science fiction.

    _____ b. I saw it three times!

    _____ c. I only went because my boyfriend made me.

    _____ d. I even bought it on DVD.

    What does the first speaker expect the second speaker to do?

    a. go to a movie with her

    b. buy a copy of the movie

    c. explain the movie to her

    d. agree with her

(continued)

3. So, do you want one of my dog's puppies?

_____ a. I've been looking for a puppy for a long time.

_____ b. They're much cuter than the puppies in the pet shop.

_____ c. My apartment doesn't allow pets.

_____ d. I'm allergic to dogs.

What does the first speaker want the second speaker to do?

a. admire her dogs

b. take a dog home

c. take care of her pets

d. not take one of her dogs

4. Can you drive tonight?

_____ a. I don't like to drive at night.

_____ b. I don't think I have enough gas.

_____ c. It would be faster than taking the train.

_____ d. Well, I don't want Tony to drive.

What are the speakers going to do tonight?

a. call a taxi

b. go somewhere together

c. stay home

d. meet Tony

5. Do you want to make dinner tonight?

_____ a. Why don't we order a pizza?

_____ b. I could make spaghetti.

_____ c. You've been working really hard. Why don't you just rest?

_____ d. Let's go out to that new Chinese place.

Where are the speakers now, probably?

a. in a restaurant

b. at work

c. at a cooking show

d. at home

C. Work with a partner. Compare your answers to Exercises A and B. What words helped you infer the information?

Listening for Tone of Voice

We can say the same thing in many different ways. The *tone of voice* we use can even give the same sentences a different meaning.

For example, in this dialogue, how do you think Speaker B feels? Unhappy? Pleased? Surprised?

A: *Jennifer can't come to the party.*

B: *Oh, really?*

We can't really know how Speaker B is feeling just by reading the dialogue. Any of the feelings listed above are possible. In the next exercises, you will hear Speaker B expressing different feelings using tone of voice.

A. 🎧 *Listen. In this example, Speaker B is sad that Jennifer can't come. Her tone of voice expresses disappointment.*

B. 🎧 *Listen again. In this example, Speaker B doesn't have a strong feeling. She doesn't really care if Jennifer can come or not, but is just answering to be polite.*

C. 🎧 *Listen again. In this example, Speaker B is happy. She is surprised, but glad, that Jennifer can't come.*

D. 🎧 *Work with a partner. Listen to all three of the dialogues again and repeat Speaker B's line. Try to use the same tone of voice.*

Then take turns reading the dialogue as shown on p. 74. Practice saying Speaker B's line in all three different ways. Can your partner tell your tone of voice?

☑ **Check Yourself**

🎧 *Listen. Circle the feeling that best describes the speaker's tone of voice.*

1. **Man:** Oh, that's just great.

   happy   surprised   angry

2. **Woman:** You did?

   surprised   upset   frightened

3. **Man:** Sure, that'll be great.

   excited   nervous   unhappy

4. **Woman:** I'm so sorry.

   kind   angry   pleased

5. **Man:** That's terrible.

   upset   sad   happy

6. **Girl:** I'm OK.

   bored   relieved   sad

PRACTICE

EXERCISE 1

A. 🎧 *Listen to each conversation. Write **T** for true or **F** for false.*

1. _____ The man thinks most modern artists can draw quite well.
2. _____ The man and woman are looking at a photograph.
3. _____ The painting is probably not very colorful.
4. _____ The artist was probably a child.
5. _____ The man is going to have a cup of coffee.

B. 🎧 *Listen again. Who likes the pictures? Check (✓) man, woman, or both.*

	Man	Woman	Both
1.	☐	☐	☐
2.	☐	☐	☐
3.	☐	☐	☐
4.	☐	☐	☐
5.	☐	☐	☐

EXERCISE 2

A. 🎧 *Listen. What is the purpose of the announcement? Circle the correct answer.*

a. to announce a change in work hours

b. to ask people to stay at work late

c. to tell workers about an event

B. 🎧 *Listen. Does the person accept the invitation? Check (✓) yes or no.*

		Yes	No
1.	Kaitlyn	☐	☐
2.	Bill	☐	☐
3.	Carol	☐	☐
4.	Jocelyn	☐	☐
5.	Max	☐	☐

■ **EXERCISE 3**

A. Vocabulary Preview *Write* **S** *if the words and expressions have a similar meaning and* **D** *if they have a different meaning.*

_____ 1. traditional – modern

_____ 2. opinion – idea

_____ 3. fancy – plain

_____ 4. wonderful – terrible

_____ 5. waste money – save money

_____ 6. fresh – new

_____ 7. safe – dangerous

_____ 8. earthquake – tornado

B. 🎧 *Listen. A reporter is interviewing people about the new town hall. Do the people like the building? Circle* **yes** *or* **no.**

1. yes   no

2. yes   no

3. yes   no

4. yes   no

5. yes   no

6. yes   no

C. 🎧 *Listen again. Write the words, phrases, or information that helped you guess the people's feelings in Exercise B. If the answer is tone of voice, write* **tone.**

1. _____

2. _____

3. _____

4. _____

5. _____

6. _____

■ **EXERCISE 4**

A. Work with a partner. On a separate piece of paper, write two indirect answers that mean "yes" and two answers that mean "no" for each question.

1. Do you like this shirt?

2. Are you a good dancer?

3. Do you want to play tennis with me?

4. Can you lend me $10.00?

5. Would you like to buy my video game system?

B. Take turns asking the questions and giving your answers. Try to use tone of voice to express feelings when you answer.

> **Applying Your Skills** For additional practice in making inferences, turn to Part 2, Unit 5, pages 88–92, and Unit 6, pages 93–97.

Lucky Numbers

Unit Warm Up

In this unit, you will listen to a talk about the meaning of numbers in different cultures.

Work with a partner. Read the cartoon and discuss the questions.

- Which person in the cartoon do you think is Hagar? Where do you think he is from?

- Where are the people? What are they doing?

- What is the problem? How does Hagar solve the problem?

LISTENING TASK

Before You Listen

A. 🎧 **Vocabulary Preview** *Listen and write the missing letters to complete the words. Then check your answers with a partner.*

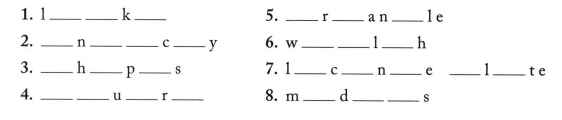

1. l ____ ____ k ____

2. ____ n ____ ____ c ____ y

3. ____ h ____ p ____ s

4. ____ ____ u ____ r ____

5. ____ r ____ a n ____ l e

6. w ____ ____ l ____ h

7. l ____ c ____ n ____ e ____ l ____ t e

8. m ____ d ____ ____ s

B. *Work with a partner. Answer the questions. Then follow the directions.*

1. What is a *lucky* number? What is an *unlucky* number?

2. For some people, *wealth* is very important. For other people, it is not. What is *wealth*?

3. Where can you see a *license plate*? What is the purpose of a *license plate*?

4. What are *medals*? Why do people get *medals*?

5. Draw four or five common shapes. Write the name of the shape below the drawing. One of your drawings should be a *square* and one should be a *triangle*.

C. **Predict** *You will hear the vocabulary from Exercise A in a short talk. Work with a partner. What do you think the talk will be about?*

While You Listen

First Listening

A. 🎧 **Main Ideas** *Listen to the first part of the talk and check (✓) the main idea.*

a. ☐ Two of the most basic shapes are the triangle and the square.

b. ☐ The number seven is lucky in many countries, and the number thirteen is unlucky.

c. ☐ Canada and the U.S. have the same lucky numbers.

B. 🎧 **Main Ideas** *Listen to the second part of the talk and check (✓) the main idea.*

a. ☐ In China, the number eight is lucky and four is unlucky.

b. ☐ The Chinese Olympic team won 42 medals at the Beijing Olympics.

c. ☐ Other Asian countries also have lucky and unlucky numbers.

Second Listening

A. 🎧 **Details** *Listen again to the first part of the talk. Then read the statements and write T for true or F for false.*

_____ 1. The number seven is lucky in many parts of the world.

_____ 2. No one knows why the number seven is so lucky.

_____ 3. In most countries, the number thirteen is lucky.

_____ 4. Friday the 30th is a bad day in many places.

_____ 5. In Greece, the number thirteen is a lucky number.

B. 🎧 **Details** *Listen again to the second part of the talk. Then complete the sentences.*

In _____ (1), numbers can be lucky or unlucky because of the way they sound. The number _____ (2) is the luckiest. That's because the word eight in Chinese and some other Asian languages sounds like the word for _____ (3). In China, some people spend a lot of money to get the number eight in their phone number or on their _____ (4). And the Beijing Olympic Games began at exactly eight minutes after eight o'clock on _____ (5) 8, 2008. That was _____ (6) on 8-8-08. Maybe that's one reason the Chinese Olympic team won a total of _____ (7) medals at the games. But China has its unlucky numbers, too. The number _____ (8) is very unlucky. That's because the word for "four" in Chinese sounds a lot like the word for _____ (9). The number four is also an unlucky number in _____ (10) and Korea.

After You Listen

■ EXERCISE 1

A. 🎧 *Listen to the questions about the talk and write short answers.*

1. _____

2. _____

3. _____

(continued)

4. _____

5. _____

6. _____

7. _____

8. _____

9. _____

B. *Compare your answers with a partner.*

■ EXERCISE 2

Work with a group. Discuss the questions.
Then share your ideas with the class.

- What do you notice about the buttons on the elevator in the picture?

- Where do you think this elevator is probably located?

- Do you have a lucky number? Do you have an unlucky one?

- What are some days or dates that are lucky or unlucky in your culture?

- Here are some things that are considered lucky or unlucky in many cultures. What about in your culture?

Unlucky

- You spill some salt.
- A black cat walks in front of you.
- You open an umbrella inside the house.
- You walk under a ladder.

Lucky

- You find a coin and pick it up.
- You carry a rabbit's foot.
- What are some other things that are lucky or unlucky in your country?

A Very Unusual Animal

Unit Warm Up

In this unit, you will hear a talk about one of the world's strangest animals.

Work with a partner. What do you know about this animal? Discuss these questions.

- What kind of animal is this?
- Where do you think it lives?
- What is special or unusual about it?

LISTENING TASK

Before You Listen

A. Vocabulary Preview *Match the words to their definitions. Use a dictionary if necessary. Then use the words to complete the sentences on the next page.*

____ **1.** mammal	a. harmful substances in the air or water
____ **2.** reptile	b. the hair of an animal
____ **3.** duck	c. a tool used to fight, like a knife or a gun
____ **4.** joke	d. a funny story or idea
____ **5.** fur	e. a kind of animal that has hair and feeds its babies with milk
____ **6.** weapon	f. afraid to be around people
____ **7.** poison	g. a type of bird that can swim
____ **8.** pollution	h. a chemical that can make someone sick or kill them
____ **9.** shy	i. a cold-blooded animal such as a snake, an alligator, or a lizard

(continued)

10. Polar bears have long white _____ that keeps them warm in cold weather.

11. Everyone was laughing at the _____ that Professor Nuñez told us.

12. Don't eat that! It has _____ in it. You'll get very sick.

13. The air in the city looks brown because of all the _____ from cars.

14. A lion is a type of _____ that lives in Africa.

15. I saw a _____ swimming in the lake near my house.

16. A turtle is a common type of _____.

17. My cat is very _____. He always runs and hides when we have visitors.

18. Dogs use their teeth as a _____ when they fight.

B. Predict *You will hear the vocabulary from Exercise A in the listening. Work with a partner. What information do you think you will hear about the animal?*

While You Listen

First Listening

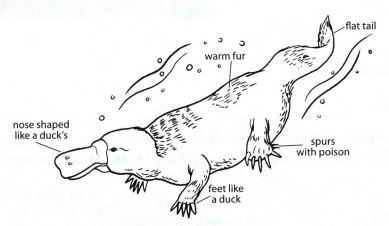

🎧 **Main Ideas** *Read the topics below. Then listen and check (✓) the topics that the speaker talks about.*

☐ what platypuses look like

☐ famous stories about platypuses

☐ who first saw the platypus

☐ where platypuses live

☐ how platypuses find food

☐ how scientists study platypuses

☐ how female platypuses take care of their babies

☐ platypuses in zoos

☐ the popularity of platypuses in Australia

Second Listening

🎧 **Details** *Listen to the talk again. Complete the sentences with information about platypuses.*

1. The platypus is a mammal, but it lays _____ .
2. Europeans first saw platypuses in the year _____ .
3. When scientists first saw drawings of platypuses, they thought the pictures were a _____ .
4. Platypuses are found in _____ Australia.
5. Female platypuses weigh about _____ as much as male platypuses.
6. Platypuses _____ during the day in holes near the water.
7. Platypuses can _____ electricity in the water that comes from other animals.
8. Platypuses don't usually hurt people because they are so _____ .
9. The female platypus lays from _____ to _____ eggs.
10. The female platypus feeds its babies with _____ .
11. There are not as many platypuses as there once were because of _____ and development.
12. You can see a picture of a platypus on the Australian _____ - cent coin.

After You Listen

■ **EXERCISE 1**

In the talk, the speaker uses comparisons to describe platypuses. Match these sentence parts to create comparisons.

_____ 1. The speaker compares platypuses with reptiles

_____ 2. Platypuses are compared with ducks

_____ 3. The speaker says male platypuses are like some snakes

_____ 4. The speaker compares a male platypus with a cat

_____ 5. Platypuses are like some fish

_____ 6. Female platypuses are like female birds

_____ 7. The speaker compares baby platypuses with beans

a. because of their feet and noses

b. because they are about the same weight.

c. because they lay eggs.

d. because of their tiny size.

e. because they use poison as a weapon.

f. because they can "feel" electricity from other animals in the water.

g. because they warm their eggs with their bodies.

Use information and vocabulary from the talk to complete the crossword puzzle.

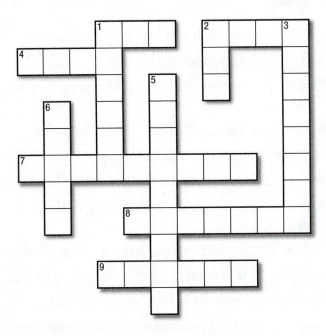

Across

1. A platypus's _____ keeps it warm and dry.

2. On the back of its leg, a platypus has a dangerous _____.

4. A _____ makes people laugh.

7. A person who works in science.

8. Animals that feed their babies with milk.

9. The _____ of a platypus is very painful to people.

Down

1. The _____ platypus is smaller than the male.

2. Afraid to be around people.

3. _____ such as snakes and turtles lay eggs.

5. The country where platypuses come from.

6. Swimming birds.

■ EXERCISE 3

Work in a group. Follow the instructions.

1. Along with the kangaroo and the koala bear, the platypus is popular in Australia and is a kind of symbol of the country. What animal or animals are popular or symbolize your country? Tell the group.

2. Think of an interesting animal. Students in your group will try to guess what animal you are thinking of by asking you yes/no or *wh-* questions.

Example

Does it live in the sea?	**No, it doesn't.**
Is it a mammal?	**Yes.**
Does it eat meat?	**No. I don't think so.**
Where does it live?	**Mostly in Africa and Asia.**
Is it big?	**Yes, very big.**
Is it an elephant?	**Yes, it is.**

Unit Warm Up

In this unit, you will hear a talk about the history of a famous song.

Work with a partner. Look at the picture. Discuss the questions.

- What are the people in the picture doing?
- What do people usually sing at this type of celebration?
- What do you think the child will do next?

LISTENING TASK

Before You Listen

A. Vocabulary Preview *Study these words and their definitions. Then use the words to complete the sentences below.*

present: something you give to someone; a gift

candle: a stick of wax with a piece of string that gives light as it burns

translate: change words from one language to another

astronaut: a person who travels in outer space

melody: the music of a song; the tune

lyrics: the words of a song

original: first; earliest

surprise: a feeling caused by something that is not expected

1. I didn't know that my friend Steve was going to visit me. When I saw him at the door, it was a big _____.

2. When I first bought this car, it was brown. I didn't like the _____ color, so I painted it blue.

3. James and Bonnie wrote this song together. James wrote the words, and Bonnie wrote the _____.

4. Erik will _____ the book from Spanish to English.

5. During the storm, the lights went out in our house, so we used _____ instead.

6. For her eighteenth birthday, Marie's parents gave her an expensive _____—a new camera.

7. I didn't understand the _____ of that song until I read them on the Internet.

8. Neil Armstrong was the first _____ to walk on the moon.

B. Predict *Work with a partner. What song do you think the talk will be about? Where do you think the song came from? How did it become popular?*

While You Listen

First Listening

🎧 **Main Ideas** *Read the statements. Then listen and check (✓) the sentences that are important ideas in the talk.*

1. ☐ Cakes and candles are an important part of birthday parties.
2. ☐ The Birthday Song is popular all over the world.
3. ☐ The original lyrics for the song were not about a birthday.
4. ☐ Mildred and Patty Hill were both kindergarten teachers.
5. ☐ People aren't sure who wrote the words for the Birthday Song.
6. ☐ A company collects money when someone sings the Birthday Song in movies or on television.

Second Listening

A. 🎧 **Details** *Listen again and circle the correct word or number to complete the sentence.*

1. People have translated the song into many languages, but even in non-English speaking countries, people often sing it in (*their own language / English*).
2. In (*1968 / 1986*), three astronauts sang the song in space.
3. The Birthday Song is over (*100 / 200*) years old.
4. The original song began, ("*Good morning* / "*Happy Birthday*) to you."
5. Today, almost no one knows the original (*title / lyrics*) for the Birthday Song.
6. The company that owns the song makes two (*thousand / million*) dollars a year, and owns the song until the year (*2020 / 2030*).

B. 🎧 **Inference** *Now listen to two people discussing a birthday party. Listen carefully to the speakers' tone of voice. If you think the sentence explains the speaker's real meaning, check (✓) Yes. If you think it does not, check (✓) No.*

	Yes	No
1. The woman thinks the man should remember Joshua.	☐	☐
2. The man is excited because he is invited to a birthday party.	☐	☐
3. The man will be happy to see Paul and Jennie.	☐	☐
4. The woman thinks the man doesn't know the words to the Birthday Song.	☐	☐

5. The woman thinks the man is joking.   ☐   ☐
6. The man believes the story is true.   ☐   ☐
7. The man believes that the police might come.   ☐   ☐

After You Listen

■ EXERCISE 1

People celebrate birthdays all over the world.

Work in groups. Discuss these questions.

1. What do people in your country do to celebrate birthdays? Are there any special foods served at those celebrations?

2. Do people in your country sing the Birthday Song? If so, do they usually sing the lyrics in English or in your own language?

3. In your country, do people sing other songs on birthdays? What do these songs say in English?

4. Tell the group about one of your favorite birthdays. How old were you? Did you receive any special presents? Who did you celebrate with? How did you celebrate?

■ EXERCISE 2

Many cultures have a traditional "coming of age" ceremony when children officially become adults. For example, in Japanese society, the ceremony is called Seijin Shiki, held at age 20. In Mexican society, young women celebrate Quinceanera when they are 15 years old.

Work in groups. Discuss these questions.

1. Do you have any similar ceremonies in your country?

2. Why do you think people all over the world celebrate "coming of age"?

■ EXERCISE 3

A. *Survey five classmates. Record when their birthdays are and how they usually celebrate.*

Classmate's Name	Birthday	How They Usually Celebrate
1.		
2.		
3.		
4.		
5.		

B. *Tell the class some interesting ways your classmates celebrate their birthdays.*

■ EXERCISE 4

Imagine that someone in your class will celebrate a birthday soon. In small groups, plan a party. Think about what you will do and what you need to bring to the party. Then share your ideas with the class.

APPLYING SKILLS

UNIT 6

The World of Fashion

Unit Warm Up

In this unit, you will listen to conversations and a talk about fashion.

Work with a partner. Discuss these questions.

- What are some examples of popular fashions right now?
- Do you usually follow new fashion styles?
- About how much money do you spend every month on clothing and accessories?
- What kinds of clothes do you like to wear?

LISTENING TASK

Before You Listen

A. Vocabulary Preview *Work with a partner. Talk about the words in the box. Are they worn by men, women, or both? Use a dictionary if necessary.*

athletic shoes	belt	blouse	boots	cap
dress	hat	sandals	scarf	shirt
skirt	socks	suit	tie	vest

B. *Use these words to label the pictures. Sometimes more than one word is possible.*

baggy	casual	fancy	formal
loose	plain	tight	

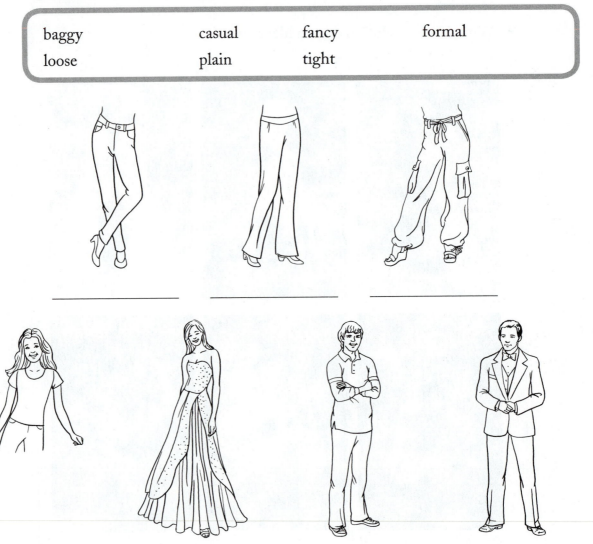

_____   _____   _____

_____   _____   _____   _____

C. **Work with a partner or group. Describe your favorite clothes. Say when and where you got them and why you like them.**

Example

My favorite jeans are old. I got them about five years ago. They're baggy.

While You Listen

First Listening

🎧 **Main Ideas** *Listen and circle the correct answer.*

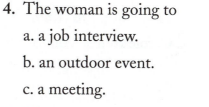

1. The woman wants the man to notice
   a. her hair.
   b. an outfit she wore before.
   c. something new.

2. The two people are
   a. friends.
   b. a mother and son.
   c. a teacher and student.

3. The announcement is about
   a. school uniforms.
   b. a clothing sale.
   c. school clothing rules.

4. The woman is going to
   a. a job interview.
   b. an outdoor event.
   c. a meeting.

5. The men are at
   a. a wedding.
   b. a clothing shop.
   c. a dinner party.

6. The man is talking about
   a. what he wants to buy.
   b. a fashion show.
   c. what people are wearing at the mall.

Second Listening

A. 🎧 **Details** *Listen again. Check (✓) the items of clothing each person mentions.*

1. ☐ hat   ☐ blouse   ☐ vest   ☐ dress
2. ☐ athletic   ☐ shirt   ☐ belt   ☐ pants
      shoes
3. ☐ dresses   ☐ skirts   ☐ shorts   ☐ caps
4. ☐ skirt   ☐ jeans   ☐ boots   ☐ suit
5. ☐ tie   ☐ shirt   ☐ hat   ☐ suit
6. ☐ suits   ☐ blouses   ☐ boots   ☐ hats

B. 🎧 **Inference** *Listen again and circle the correct information.*

1. a. The man (*notices / doesn't notice*) something new.

   b. The man (*likes / doesn't care about*) her hat.

   c. The woman (*is / isn't*) angry at him.

2. a. The mother is unhappy about her son's (*clothes / music*).

   b. His pants are too (*tight / loose*).

   c. He (*will / won't*) take off his belt after he leaves the house.

3. a. This information is (*new / old*).

   b. Students might try to wear clothes that are too (*tight / short*).

   c. Sports uniforms (*include / don't*) include shorts.

4. a. Carole thinks "comfortable" clothes are too (*loose / casual*).

   b. Carole thinks her friend's dress is (*appropriate / not appropriate*).

   c. Lindsey (*trusts / doesn't trust*) her friend's advice.

5. a. The man (*is / isn't*) relaxed.

   b. The tie is (*too tight / just right*).

   c. He (*is used to / isn't used to*) wearing a suit.

6. a. People (*would / would not*) look fashionable in brown pants this fall.

   b. Spring boots were probably (*long / short*).

   c. The new color for hats is probably (*brown / another color*).

After You Listen

■ EXERCISE 1

***What do you think a man and woman should wear for these occasions?
Make notes. Then share your ideas with a group.***

   a. a job interview at a software company

   b. your best friend's birthday party at a restaurant

   c. as a guest at a wedding

   d. the first day of a university class

   e. a walk in the park

■ EXERCISE 2

Work in a small group. Discuss whether you like the fashions in the pictures. Explain why or why not.

Example

> *A: I don't like these pants. They're too baggy.*
>
> *B: Really? I like them. I have some baggy pants. They're very comfortable.*

■ EXERCISE 3

Discuss these sayings and opinions with a group. What do they mean? Which ones do you agree with?

1. Clothes make the man.

2. People seldom notice old clothes if you wear a big smile.

3. When in doubt, wear red.

4. Women usually love what they buy, but hate most of what is in their closets.

5. It's always the badly dressed people who are the most interesting.

6. Expensive clothes are a waste of money.

PART 3

Listening for Pleasure

Unit Warm Up

In this unit, you will listen to excerpts (short clips) from TV shows.

Work with a partner. Discuss the questions.

- What kinds of TV shows are these?
- Name some similar shows you know. Do you watch them?

Introduction

Are you a TV fan? Do you ever watch shows in English? Watching TV in English can be a great way to learn new vocabulary and hear the sound of natural spoken English. Watching people's faces and body language, and paying attention to the story or situation can help you understand even more.

Work in groups. Discuss the questions.

1. How many hours of television do you watch every week?
2. What types of shows do you like? Are there any types you don't like?
3. What is easy about watching TV or movies in English? What is challenging?

LISTENING TASK

Before You Listen

Work with a partner. Look at these types of TV shows. What might you see or hear on each one?

cartoon	cooking show	drama	news show	science fiction	sports show
comedy	documentary	game show	reality show	soap opera	talk show

While You Listen

First Listening

🎧 **Main Idea** *Listen to excerpts from six television programs. Number them in the order you hear them.*

_____ soap opera _____ commercial _____ science fiction

_____ news show _____ talk show _____ game show

Second Listening

A. 🎧 **Details** *Listen again and check (✓) the words and expressions you hear in each program.*

1. ☐ alien ☐ unknown ☐ space ☐ weapon

2. ☐ let me introduce ☐ our first guest tonight ☐ tell us about ☐ please show us

3. ☐ our next category ☐ contestant number 2 ☐ you just won ☐ the winner is

4. ☐ our top story tonight ☐ film at 11:00 ☐ our reporter ☐ on the scene

5. ☐ tastes great ☐ limited time offer ☐ best-selling ☐ it's a great value, too

6. ☐ doesn't love you ☐ lost the money ☐ mysterious stranger ☐ Please go.

B. 🎧 **Inference** *Listen again and circle the correct answer.*

1. Officer Ryan thinks ____.

   a. they should act quickly

   b. they need more information

   c. they should fight the alien

2. Brad thinks the plot of Katie's new movie is ____.

   a. not unusual

   b. very funny

   c. surprising

3. The host is ____ when the woman answers the question correctly.

   a. surprised

   b. pleased

   c. unhappy

4. The reporter's tone is ____.

   a. excited

   b. afraid

   c. serious

5. Zippy has trouble remembering ____.

   a. what he has for breakfast

   b. the interviewer's name

   c. what the commercial is for

6. The second woman thinks that Alberto ____.

   a. isn't going to get married

   b. loves Emily

   c. is very rich

After You Listen

■ EXERCISE 1

Work in groups. Think about TV commercials. Discuss the questions.

1. What are some things you like about TV commercials? What do you dislike?

2. What are some examples of commercials that you like or dislike?

3. What are some qualities of "good" TV commercials?

4. Describe a TV commercial you have seen. What product was it for? What happened during the commercial? Do you think it was a good commercial? Why or why not?

■ EXERCISE 2

Work with a partner. Look at these common expressions from TV commercials. Write P by the ones that are about price and Q by the ones about quality.

_____ 1. 25% off!

_____ 2. Now on sale!

_____ 3. Better than the others!

_____ 4. Only the best!

_____ 5. Big savings!

_____ 6. Made to last!

_____ 7. Now better than ever!

_____ 8. Great value!

_____ 9. Tastes great!

_____ 10. Buy the best!

■ EXERCISE 3

A. *A storyboard is a plan for a TV show, movie, or commercial. Look at the storyboard pictures and read the plan for the Speed-M-Up gum commercial.*

Interviewer introduces "Zippy" Joe Morrow

Interviewer: "How do you get ready for a race?"

Zippy: "I always chew Speed-M-Up gum!"

Zippy: "Speed-M-Up gum tastes great. It helps me win every race!"

Interviewer: "Speed-M-Up gum is better than the others. And it's a great value!"

Interviewer: "Chew the best. Speed-M-Up gum."

B. 🎧 **Listen to the commercial for Speed-M-Up gum. Did the commercial follow the storyboard? What was different?**

C. *Work with a partner or group. Imagine you work for the same company. Think of a product you want to sell. Take notes.*

Product Name:_____	**Price:**_____
Special Features:_____	

D. **Create a simple storyboard for your commercial featuring your product from Exercise C. Practice it a few times. Then perform it for the class!**

UNIT 2

Two Folktales

In this unit, you will hear two folktales: *The Fisherman* and *Stone Soup*.

Work with a partner. Discuss the questions.

- What are some reasons people tell stories out loud?
- What kind of stories do they usually tell?
- When was the last time you listened to a story? Describe the experience.

Introduction

Folktales are simple, traditional stories that usually teach a lesson about life or emphasize an important value, such as honesty, kindness, patience, or hard work. Folktales vary from country to country, of course, but every culture has some type of folktale, and there are common themes even in stories from very different places.

Work in groups. Discuss the questions.

- Think about common folktales you know. What kinds of characters do they have? For example, a poor farmer, a princess, a magician, etc.

- What common topics or themes do folktales have? For example, a poor man gets rich; a poor woman marries a prince, etc.

- What are some reasons that people tell and read folktales?

LISTENING TASK

STORY 1 The Fisherman

Before You Listen

A. Predict *Work with a partner. Look back at the picture on p. 105. What do you think this folktale will be about?*

B. *Work with a partner. Find these things in the picture on p. 105.*

| a fisherman | a dock | a harbor | a fleet of boats | a canning factory |

While You Listen

Part 1

🎧 **Main Idea** *Listen and check (✓) the correct answer.*

1. Who are the characters?

   ☐ two brothers   ☐ two strangers   ☐ a boss and his employee

2. How many fish did the fisherman catch?

   ☐ two   ☐ four   ☐ six

3. How long did he fish?

   ☐ part of the day   ☐ all day   ☐ two days

Part 2

🎧 **Main Idea** *Listen and then complete the summary.*

The businessman told the fisherman to catch as many _____
                                                                (1)
as possible, then sell the extra fish for some _____, and then
                                                         (2)
buy a bigger _____, and to continue until he had a whole fleet
                    (3)
of _____.
          (4)

Part 3

🎧 **Details** *Listen and circle the correct word or phrase to complete the sentence.*

1. The businessman tells the fisherman to build his own (*supermarket / canning factory*).

2. He says the fisherman could move to (*a big city / a peaceful village*).

3. He says it might take (*5 or 10 / 15 or 20*) years.

Part 4

🎧 *Listen. Then work with a partner or group. Discuss the questions.*

1. What does the businessman tell the fisherman he can do?

2. Why is the ending of the story funny?

3. What do you think the fisherman will tell the businessman?

After You Listen

■ **EXERCISE 1**

Work with a partner. What lesson do you think this story teaches? Discuss your ideas and write the lesson in one or two sentences. Then share your ideas with the class. Do other students have the same ideas?

■ EXERCISE 2

A. Work with a partner. Read these popular English sayings. Discuss what they mean. Check (✓) the ones that you think the story shows.

1. ☐ All work and no play makes Jack a dull boy.

2. ☐ Money can't buy happiness.

3. ☐ One man's meat is another man's poison.

4. ☐ The best things in life are free.

5. ☐ Failing to plan is planning to fail.

6. ☐ If a job is worth doing, it is worth doing well.

B. Work with a partner or group. Which sayings in Exercise 2A do you agree with? What sayings in your language are similar?

■ EXERCISE 3

A. Read the list of reasons that people work. How important are these reasons to you?

- **Draw a star (*) by the ones you think are very important.**
- **Check (✓) the ones you think are somewhat important.**
- **Write an X by the ones you think are not important.**

_____ to get money

_____ because your family expects it

_____ because your society or culture expects it

_____ because you enjoy it

_____ just to have something to do

_____ to give something to your community or the world

_____ because you have a special skill or talent

another reason: _____

another reason: _____

B. Share your answers to Exercise A with a partner or group. Explain your choices.

STORY 2 STONE SOUP

Before You Listen

A. Predict *Talk with the class. In this story, a traveler with no money stops in town to get something to eat. How do you think he will get food without any money?*

Example
·········

Maybe he will ask people for food.

B. Study these words and expressions from the story and their meanings.

once upon a time: a long time ago; a very common way for folktales to begin

stingy: someone who doesn't like to spend money or give things to other people; the opposite of *generous*

barn: a building for farm animals such as horses and cows

no matter: an expression similar to *It's not important.*

It's a shame. an expression similar to *It's too bad.*

fit for a king: very special; good enough for a king

While You Listen

Part 1

A. 🎧 **Listen to the first part of the story. Then work with a partner and complete the summary.**

There was an old _____ who lived alone. She had money, but she
            (1)

was _____. One day, a _____ came to her house.
            (2)   (3)

He wanted two things: _____ and _____. The man
                              (4)   (5)

said he could make soup with _____. The woman said he could sleep
                                      (6)

in the _____.
            (7)

B. Talk with a partner. What do you think the woman will say next? Write your guess.

_____

_____

Part 2

A. 🎧 **Listen to the next part of the story. Did you guess correctly in Exercise 1B? Circle the correct words below.**

The stone looked (*special / ordinary*). The man put the stone (*in / next to*) the pot of soup. In the pot, he put some (*water / meat*). The man said the soup was (*good / not very good*).

B. *Talk with a partner. What do you think the woman will say? What will happen next? Write your guess.*

_____

_____

Part 3

A. 🎧 *Listen to the next part of the story. Did you guess correctly? Talk with a partner. What food got added to the soup? Explain in your own words how the man got that food.*

B. *Talk with a partner. What do you think the woman will do next? Will the two people enjoy their meal? Write your guesses.*

_____

_____

Part 4

🎧 *Listen to the end of the story. Did you guess correctly? Check (✓) the sentences that are true.*

_____ 1. There wasn't enough food for dinner.

_____ 2. The soup was delicious.

_____ 3. The man slept in the house.

_____ 4. The man made breakfast with his stone.

_____ 5. The woman served breakfast to the man.

_____ 6. The man gave the woman a gold coin.

_____ 7. The woman gave the man a gold coin.

_____ 8. The woman's attitude changed.

_____ 9. The woman learned a new cooking skill.

_____ 10. The stone was magic.

After You Listen

Work with a group. Discuss the questions.

1. What is the lesson of the story?

2. How can you apply that lesson in your own life? Think of one example to share with the class.

Unit Warm Up

In this unit, you will listen to a radio talk show where people call in on the telephone to talk to an expert.

Work with a partner. Look at the pictures. Discuss the questions.

- In which of these places have you gone online?
- What do you use to go online (a desktop computer, a laptop, a cell phone)?
- What kinds of websites do you use most often?

Introduction

You can hear many kinds of things on the radio—music, talk shows, and news shows. With the Internet, you can go online and listen to radio stations from around the world. This makes it easy to find lots of things to listen to in English. On radio station websites, you can even get podcasts about topics you're interested in, so you can listen to English anywhere!

Work in groups. Discuss the questions.

1. Do you ever listen to the radio? When and where do you listen? What do you like to listen to?

2. Think about radio talk shows in your country. What kinds of topics are popular?

3. Have you ever called a radio talk show? If so, describe the experience.

4. What is easy about listening to the radio in English? What is challenging?

LISTENING TASK

Before You Listen

A. Vocabulary Preview *Complete the crossword puzzle with words from the box.*

account	employer	privacy
click on	engine	spam
employee	illegal	surf

Across

1. Something that is against the law is _____.

4. _____ means being alone, unseen, or secret.

7. An _____ is the company or person someone works for.

8. I like to _____ the Internet and find new websites.

9. Google is a popular search _____.

Down

2. An _____ is someone who works for someone else.

3. Email from advertisers that you don't want is called _____.

5. I only have one email _____.

6. Do you ever _____ links you see online?

(continued)

B. Use the words from Exercise A to complete the sentences.

1. I'm very worried about Internet _____. I don't want anyone to read my email!

2. A lot of people _____ the Internet while they are at work.

3. It should be _____ to buy things on the Internet if you are under 18 years old.

4. I never _____ ads on Web pages. I just don't trust them!

5. I really hate _____ messages. I get about ten of them in my email inbox every day!

6. Does your _____ give a laptop to everyone in the office?

7. I always use the same search _____ to look for information online.

8. When did you start working for this _____?

9. Please use this new email address. I don't have that old _____ anymore.

10. My company posts a photo of each _____ on its website.

C. Check (✓) the sentences that are true for you. Then compare your answers with a partner.

☐ I have a desktop computer or a laptop at home.

☐ I can check my email or go online with my cell phone.

☐ I have more than one email account.

☐ I don't think online shopping is safe.

☐ I often spend more than three hours online in one day.

(continued)

☐ I sometimes chat online.

☐ I worry about Internet safety.

☐ I don't like ads on the Internet.

☐ I have my own Web page or blog.

☐ I use networking sites, such as Facebook or LinkedIn.

D. Work with a partner. Discuss the questions.

1. How much time do you spend online in an average week?

2. What are two things you like and two things you dislike about using the Internet?

3. What are some things that you think are unsafe to do online (for example, post your home address)?

While You Listen

First Listening

🎧 **Main Idea** *Listen to a radio talk show about Internet privacy. What problem does each person have? Circle the correct answer.*

1. Jerry is upset because

   a. he can't read his personal email at work.

   b. he gets too many personal emails at work.

   c. his boss can read his personal email.

2. Emily has a problem with too

   a. many online shopping sites.

   b. much spam.

   c. many emails each day.

3. Anna is asking about

   a. putting personal photos online.

   b. what search engine is best.

   c. how to make a personal Web site.

4. Adam doesn't like

   a. online ads.

   b. reading online.

   c. using his credit card online.

Second Listening

A. 🎧 **Details** *Listen again and complete the sentences from the show.*

1. **Jerry:** Uh, hi, Carl, I have a question about email _____.

   Carl: Well, they just want to know that you're not involved in any _____ activity.

   Carl: And don't check it at work, either—if you don't have _____ access at home, use an Internet café, or try the public library.

2. **Emily:** I have one of those free Web-based email _____, like you were just talking about with the other caller.

   Carl: If your email account offers _____ protection, then make sure that's turned on.

3. **Anna:** Well, I have a _____ Web site, you know?

   Carl: And… have you hidden it from _____?

4. **Adam:** I like to _____ the Internet, you know?

   Carl: Well, you see, Adam, those ads help pay for the _____ that you're looking at.

B. 🎧 **Inference** *Listen again. What tone of voice is used by the callers? Circle the correct word.*

1. **Jerry:**   happy   relieved   nervous
2. **Emily:**   frustrated   excited   sad
3. **Anna:**   not serious   upset   surprised
4. **Adam:**   angry   bored   embarrassed

After You Listen

■ EXERCISE 1

Read the situation. Then discuss the questions with a group.

Karen Black of Boston was fired from her job because she spent too much time writing personal email at work. She didn't know that her boss was reading her email.

1. Should employers be allowed to read their employee's email? Should they have to tell employees in advance?

2. Should teenagers be allowed to have email accounts without their parents' OK? Should children?

3. Should companies be allowed to sell your name and email address to advertisers without telling you? Is it OK if they do tell you?

4. Do you think it's safe to give out your credit card number or bank account number online?

5. Do you think it's safe to put personal information online, such as your name, address, or photo on a social networking site? Why or why not?

■ EXERCISE 2

A. *Survey your classmates' Internet habits. Check how often each person does each action.*

How often do you...	Very Often	Sometimes	Not Too Often	Never
buy products online?				
post a comment or opinion online?				
post personal information online?				
use an Internet search engine?				
give out your name and email address on a Web site?				
click on advertisements that you find on Web pages?				
take Internet quizzes or surveys, or enter contests?				
answer spam?				
go to an Internet café?				
email someone in another country?				

B. *Work with a partner. Discuss your survey results. Write a short report (1–2 paragraphs) about whether you think your classmates practice good Internet safety. Do you have any advice? Present your report to the class.*

Credits

Cover photos: Shutterstock.com

Page 13 (left) David Mager, (right) FogStock/Alamy; p. 36 Ethel Davies/ImageState; p. 57 Dreamstime.com; p. 60 Dreamstime.com; p. 64 (left) Shutterstock.com, (right) Phototake Inc./Alamy; p. 69 (all) Shutterstock.com; p.71 (top left) Shutterstock.com, (top right) Bigstock.com, (bottom left) iStockphoto.com, (bottom right) iStockphoto.com; p. 79 Used with the permission of King Features Syndicate and the Cartoonist Group. License 210-198; p. 82 Dreamstime.com; p. 83 Fotolia.com; p. 88 Corbis Super RF/Alamy; p. 91 Jeremy Woodhouse/Photolibrary.com; p. 93 (all) Shutterstock.com; p. 97 (left) Dreamstime.com, (middle left) iStockphoto.com, (middle right) Shutterstock.com, (right) Iain Masterton/Alamy; p. 100 (left) ABC/Photofest, (middle) Scott Gries/Getty Images, (right) ABC/Photofest; p. 103 Shutterstock.com; p. 111 (all) Shutterstock.com.